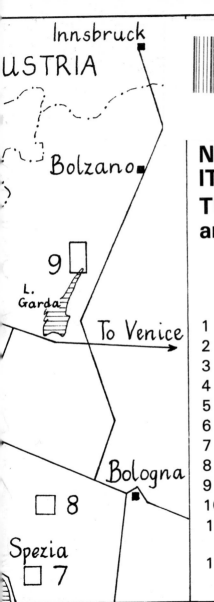

C000140660

NORTHERN ITALY
The climbing areas

1	MACHABY
2	VALLE DELL'ORCO
3	LA VALLE SUSA
4	ROCCA SBARUA
5	FINALE
6	MUZZERONE
7	MONTE PROCINTO
8	BISMANTOVA
9	ARCO
10	THE LECCO AREA
11	MELLO AND THE VALTELLINA
12	BALMANOSLESCA

Innsbruck

AUSTRIA

Bolzano

9

L. Garda

To Venice

Bologna

8

Spezia

7

ITALIAN ROCK

Selected rock-climbs in Northern Italy

ITALIAN ROCK

Selected rock-climbs in Northern Italy

by Al Churcher

Maps and Diagrams by Jill Churcher

CICERONE PRESS
MILNTHORPE, CUMBRIA

Spiaggia delle Lucertole, Arco

Published by Cicerone Press 1988
ISBN 0 902363 93 X

ACKNOWLEDGEMENTS

My thanks to everyone who has assisted in the production of this guidebook. *Alp* magazine for permission to use the information on Toblino, and for a great deal of valuable research material. Stella and John Adams, Paul Dearden, Roland and Mark Edwards for route notes and checking sections of manuscript. Pete Gomersall for extensive help with the Finale and Arco sections. Mike Mortimer for information on Arco. Ian Smith for printing the black and white photographs, and Walt Unsworth for believing that holidaying British climbers don't only climb in France.

Above all to three Italian friends: Davide Battistella, Renato Giustetto and Paolo Mazzarelli. Davide for his help with Arco and for the bulk of the Muzzerone section, and Renato and Paola for the information, help and encouragement that they have given me over the years. The fact that this guidebook exists is due in no small part to them - and to the small fortune they must have spent on postage.

Finally to my wife Jill for both the long hours spent holding my ropes, and for her work as illustrator and proof-reader. She didn't quite realize what she had taken on when she agreed to 'do a few drawings', but the results have more than justified her care and commitment - and we're still on speaking terms....

CONTENTS

PREFACE

In the six years we have been climbing in Italy there has been a revolution in styles and standards. When we first visited the Mello Valley in 1982 the Alpine ethic still ruled; it was quite normal for pitches of straightforward 5a jamming to be climbed at A1, and the sound of climbers weighed down with hammers, pegs and etriers clanking past our tent soon became familiar. This is not to denigrate Italian climbing. Italians were - and to a large extent still are - a nation of alpinists, and the free-climbing ethic that had already worked across France and Germany, simply took a little longer to reach Italy. Of course hard free climbs - such as the bold friction climbs of Antonio Boscacci - existed before the 80's. Nuova Dimensione, Italy's first Grade VII, is a good example. First climbed in 1977 it remains a serious lead at E2 5b. This gives some justification to the local climbers' resistance to the bolt, and Mello remains an area where one can still experience long, serious run-outs. It is interesting to note that a pitch of jamming was not recorded in Italy until 1978 - Bonelli's first free ascent of 'Mistero' in Valle dell'Orco, although this was pre-dated by the roadside boulder problem of the Fessura Kosterlitz.

Today there is a whole new generation of free-climbers with ethics every bit as strict as their British counterparts. Standards have risen accordingly; of almost 400 routes described in this volume, over 40 are graded E5 and above, with a number of 7a. The advent of 'Spit-rock' in the early 80's, with bolts placed by abseil - often with the use of power drills - opened up new areas of rock and accelerated this rise. Easily accessible limestone cliffs such as Striature Nere, Toblino, and parts of Finale, have been rapidly developed to give very testing routes in an essentially non-serious atmosphere, similar to that of Pen Trwyn and Malham. The movement spread to mountain crags, and every few months another neglected area previously spurned for its old-fashioned classics is re-discovered. Add whole areas such as Muzzerone where not a single climb existed until a few years ago, and Italy's potential is enormous.

But for myself and many others it will perhaps be the long granite climbs of Orco and Mello that are the jewels in Italy's crown. Certainly there is little on this side of the Atlantic to rival the experience offered by routes such as Luna Nascente, Kundalini, Itaca/Tempi Moderni or Diedro Nanchez. Each of these offers from six hundred to over a thousand feet of memorable climbing in magnificent surroundings, and all are within reach of the average climber.

It would be a pity to visit Italy just for the climbing. Many of the cliffs lie in beautiful alpine valleys, and the pleasures of strolling through the ancient streets of small towns and villages often remain long after the elation of success on a difficult route has faded. Each area has its own cuisine, and seeking out the delights of the village *trattorie* is a pleasure not to be missed. Italian wines have a quality and variety far beyond the Chiantis and Lambruscos normally imported to Britain. There is much to be said for the wines of all the areas contained in this volume, but certainly those of Piemonte should not be missed - Barolo, Barbera, Dolcetto, Nebbiolo - the names roll off the tongue almost as easily as the rich red liquid slides down it.

Finally, and for me the greatest pleasure, the Italian people themselves. We have been given warm beds in the middle of the night when our tent has been blown flat, camped on farmers' meadows and had weeks of hospitality with no question of payment, people have driven miles out of their way to direct us - in short we have met with nothing but friendship and hospitality. The Italian people are unbeatable for their warmth - the least we can do is to respect their land. In popular areas such as Finale we are only a small part of the armies of continental climbers who invade Italy every year, but we can ensure that we are as unobtrusive and *sympatico* as possible. And try and learn at least a few words of the language - the way people's faces light up at even the most mangled attempt at ordering groceries or a meal in Italian will be ample reward.

INTRODUCTION

General

This guidebook contains information on twelve of the best and most highly developed free-climbing areas in Northern Italy, several of which are making their first guidebook appearance. The Dolomites, with their more alpine nature, have been deliberately excluded, although the long climbs on Arco's Cima Colodri give something of the flavour of dolomitic climbing. However, many of Arco's climbs are short, hard and on perfect rock, an example of a new style of climbing now developing in parts of the Dolomites -notably at San Martino, home ground of Manolo, Italy's most famous rock star. Other potentially interesting cliffs of the east coast of the Veneto have also been excluded.

The majority of cliffs described here are to be found in the valleys of Piemonte and Lombardia, their proximity to the French and Swiss borders making them ideal destinations for storm harassed alpinists. The mountain areas of Mello and Orco receive their share of bad weather, but the crags dry quickly and the weather is usually better than further north. The most settled weather conditions are generally in late spring and early autumn, and being cooler than summer these are also the best periods for both the lower altitudes of Arco, Lecco, Machaby and the Susa Valley, and the Mediterranean areas of Finale and Muzzerone, although here, climbing takes place all year round.

Having said that, the vast majority of our Italian climbing has been in July and August, and although we have often had to show extreme stoicism in the face of a baking sun, we have rarely lost more than a few days to rain. Even the appalling wet summer of 1984 cost us little more than one week out of five, and these months tend to have the added bonus of virtually empty crags.

Locations

Detailed access and approach notes will be found in the area introductions and cliff descriptions, which should be used in conjunction with the appropriate maps accompanying the text. Except where otherwise stated all directions are given facing into the cliff.

Equipment

Most areas are well equipped with in-situ protection - pegs or bolts. Older face climbs in some areas were often equipped with hammered bolts - a hole was drilled into the rock and a round shafted peg hammered in. To differentiate these from the more common expansion bolts or 'spits', I have used the term 'peg-bolt', as it seems that there is no existing English phrase. A good number of karabiners and quick-draws, plus a few slings, nuts and/or Friends etc. will be sufficient for most routes. Where a climb requires a full rack of nuts etc., this is generally stated in the text. Fifty metre ropes have become the norm in recent years, and are certainly recommended, not least for the greater safety and convenience when abseiling.

Gradings

British technical and E grades have been used almost throughout. In addition to their accepted value, technical grades allow convenient comparisons to be made with the French grades becoming increasingly popular in Italy, and discussion with many British climbers has revealed that most would prefer to have E grades - if only to have something to argue about after a route! Gradings are always a matter for intense debate, and even today's 'guidebook by committee' do not always satisfy everyone. Although where possible I have cross-checked my gradings with other British or Italian climbers, there were numerous routes where I knew of no other British ascensionists to discuss E grades with. In any case, grades will always be subjective, and should never be taken as more than a guide to the difficulty of a climb.

Although I have personally climbed a high proportion of the routes in most areas, there is one area - Muzzerone - where I have done very little, and two others - Striature Nere and the Gola di Toblino - nothing at all. Almost all of the climbs concerned are bolt-protected single or two pitch routes, and as (a) many would argue these are the type of climb which least need E grades, and (b) I know of no other Brit who has visited the areas concerned, these routes have not been given E grades.

On the use of aid, in a few cases overall quality has been given precedence over ethical purity; usually on long routes with one or two sections of a disparately high standard. In such cases grades have been given for both aided and free ascents.

GRADES OF DIFFICULTY - Table of Comparison

ENGLISH	FRENCH	UIAA	USA	BELGIUM	AUSTRALIA
4 a	4 +	V	5,6	IV	15
4 b	5 –	V+	5,7	IV+	16
4 c	5	VI–	5,8		17
5 a	5 +	VI	5,9	V–	18
5 b	6 a	VI+	5,10 a	V	19
		VII–	5,10 b	V+	20
5 c	6 b	VII	5,10 c	VI–	21
		VII+	5,10 d		
6 a	6 c	VIII–	5,11 a	VI	22
			5,11 b		23
6 b	7 a	VIII	5,11 c	VI+	24
		VIII+	5,11 d		25
6 c	7 b	IX–	5,12 a	VII–	26
		IX	5,12 b		27
7 a	7 c		5,12 c		28
		IX+	5,12 d		29
	8 a	X–	5,13 a		30
					31
	‹ 8 b	X	5.13 b		

Nomenclature

The Italian area, cliff and route names have been used throughout, although the prefix 'Via' has been dropped from routes. Translations have been given for some interesting or unusual names.

Maps and Other Guidebooks

Where they exist, details of definitive Italian guidebooks accompany each area, and a brief glossary is included to assist their use. Two 'Hard Rock' type volumes by Alessandro Gogna are also of interest. The first covers principally the area of this guidebook, the second the cliffs of Aosta and Piemonte with some interesting pictures of a number of routes described here.

   Cento Nuovi Mattini. Pub Zanichelli 1981

   Rock Story. Pub Melograno Edizioni 1983

The magazine *Alp* is an invaluable source of information on the Italian climbing scene.

The following excellent 1:200,000 Touring Club Italiano road maps have been particularly useful, although unfortunately the first 2 overlap considerably:

   Piemonte, Valle d'Aosta (for Machaby, Orco, Susa, Sbarua and Finale).

   Liguria (for Monaco, part of Susa, Sbarua, Finale, Muzzerone, Bismantova and Procinto).

   Lombardia (for Lecco, Mello and Arco).

   Veneto, Friuli etc. (for Arco, Dolomites and E coast).

For more detailed information the appropriate 1:50,000 Kompass Carta Turistica sheets are of value.

All these maps can be obtained from: McCarta Ltd., 122 Kings Cross Road, London WC1X 9DS. Tel: 01 278 8276. They offer a very good postal service.

They are also available from Edward Stanford Ltd., 27A Floral Street, London WC2E 9LP. Tel: 01 836 1321.

Camping and Access

As many of the cliffs described are either in National Parks or surrounded by heavily cultivated land, rough camping is often difficult. Campsite descriptions are included for each area, but for those who prefer more secluded spots it is often possible to obtain permission to camp on small hay-meadows, particularly when these have just been cut. Please obtain permission first - what to you is just a patch of rough grass, may be an important crop to local people. As an alternative to camping, cheap rooms can often be found for as little as 10,000 lire per person per night, although in tourist areas such as Liguria it is necessary to look to the small villages. Taking breakfast and evening meal at the same establishment can often produce the best deal. In October '87 we obtained an inclusive price of 25,000 lire - the superb three course evening meal including wine and coffee.

In recent years access problems have mainly occurred at cliffs surrounded by vines, e.g. Gruviera (Machaby) and parts of Arco. Vines are of great value so treat them with respect. Thoughtless parking and disposal of litter and body waste also do little to enhance the reputation of climbers.

Thefts from cars are an increasing problem everywhere, and although in my experience the situation in Italy is not as bad as that in Provence, it is as well to be security minded when parking. Always stow everything possible out of sight in the boot, do not leave money and other valuables in the car, and where possible always park in sight of houses etc. The main car parking area under the main cliff of Machaby has become a favourite place for thieves, and it is probably safer to park near the white house below Gruviera.

Further Information
The author welcomes new information on the region from climbers with first-hand experience, comments on existing grades, routes etc. These should be addressed to the author via the publisher.

MACHABY

From the Aosta-Turin autostrada, the vine-clad hillsides of the Aosta valley are punctuated by rocks and crumbling castles. The most impressive cliff is a great dome-shaped mass of rosy-yellow gneiss just south of Verres. This is Corma di Machaby, nearly 1,000 feet of solid glacier smoothed slabs, interrupted only by the large tree-covered ledges or gardens which provide useful identification features. The central and largest garden (Giardino di Centro) lies at one-third height, although due to foreshortening it appears to be at about halfway up the cliff. Slightly left and lower is the left-hand garden, while logically enough, the right-hand lies above and rightwards.

South-facing, and with a base altitude of only 200 metres, the long climbs of the main cliff are best in spring or autumn, but at the foot of the main cliff are two areas of shorter climbs which provide excellent climbing throughout much of the year. With its easy access from the motorway, Machaby is an ideal stopping-off point en route to Finale etc., and as it is only an hour and a half's drive to Orco, it can provide a welcome sunny retreat in periods of bad mountain weather.

Access and Approach to Main Cliff
If approaching from the north (i.e. Switzerland or France), take the Verres exit from the Aosta-Turin autostrada. Continue south along the road parallel to this until the cliffs appear on the left, just after you pass under a flyover. Obvious parking area at the bend in the road below the main crag. However, because of thieves it is probably better to park near the white house below Gruviera. (Coming from the south, take the Pont St. Martin exit.) The access path leads first rightwards and then zig-zags over slabs and ruined terraces to the foot of the main cliff. Twenty minutes - waymarked in orange paint.

Camping, Guidebooks etc.
As the land around Machaby is heavily cultivated with vines right up to the foot of the cliffs, it is very difficult to camp close to the crag, although discreet bivouacs are possible in good weather. However, the campsite at Quincinetto (about ten miles south, beyond Pont St. Martin and signposted on the motorway), was reasonably priced in 1984.

The old towns of Verres and Pont St. Martin provide interesting shopping expeditions; and, as many local people speak it as a first language, an opportunity to practise your French.

A thin booklet of topos was produced by Grivel in 1985. All routes have numbers painted below which correspond to those used in the booklet, and most have names painted as well.

CORMA DI MACHABY - The Main Cliff

The rock here is remarkably compact, and except for the obvious corners the scouring of the glaciers has left few cracks for nuts or pegs. Consequently, on the long classics of the 70's which make up the bulk of the routes, the protection tends to be rather spaced and difficult to arrange - particularly on the easier pitches, with peg-bolts on the blank sections on the harder ones. It is therefore advisable to climb a little within one's usual standard for the first route here, though the more recent (and generally harder) climbs are equipped with spits. Although mostly of a slabby nature, the climbing is principally on small holds, rarely relying purely on friction. The constant noise of the autostrada is an unfortunate accompaniment to the climbing, but it does tend to merge into the background after a while.

Descent. Most of the routes can be abseiled - the line of Diedro being particularly useful for climbs on the right-hand side of the face. However it is worth visiting the summit at least once, for just behind is the peaceful hamlet of Machaby and its friendly cafe. From here an easy walk of an hour returns you to the road - carry trainers and leave sacs in the car.

Diretta del Banano e Galion   310m HVS 5a
   Lorenzi et al '77 and '79
A classic combination giving a fairly direct way up the left-hand side of the cliff. With the exception of a few moves on the first pitch, and the second pitch above the left-hand garden, the climbing is mainly of VS standard, but with sparse protection.

CORMA DI MACHABY

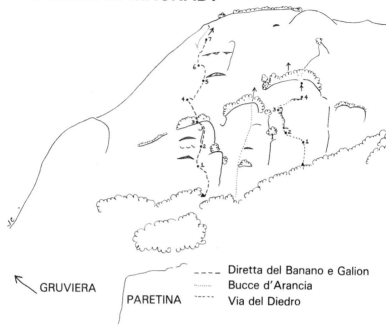

↖ GRUVIERA

PARETINA

---- Diretta del Banano e Galion
.... Bucce d'Arancia
- - - - - Via del Diedro

Start at a clean pillar to the right of the left-hand garden, and left
of the gully of the original start. 'Banano' painted on rock.

1.   30m 5a. After an awkward mantel to reach the first peg, and
a delicate step up above, trend generally left to a small ledge.
(Voglia di Tenerezza reaches this point direct at 5c, and continues
by another pitch of 5b.)

2.   30m 4c. Slightly left, then back right to a ledge.

3.   45m 4c. Good climbing leads direct to an area of ledges at
30m. Either belay here, or continue easily leftwards to the left-
hand garden.

4.   30m 4b. Follow a diagonal ramp and flake leftwards to a
ledge.

5.   30m 5a. Go slightly right and bridge up a strangely shattered
groove, well protected by several bolts.

6.   35m 4c. The obvious traverse line of Banano leads horizontally rightwards under the roof above. Ignore this and climb directly

up to the left of the roof, finally traversing left to a stance on a small ledge.

7.   45m 4c. Direct to a tree at 15m (belay) and taking the overhang above on its exteme left, continue more easily by slabs to the right of an open groove to a good stance.

Abseil from here, or continue by another 70 metres of easy climbing (2 to 3 pitches) to the summit.

Gatta da Pelare   120m E4 6b
Azzalea '82

Well equipped with spits for protection and belays, this route takes the reddish slab beneath the left-hand side of the central garden. Start immediately right of the corner of Banano.

1.   35m 5a. Climb the vertical wall, fairly direct at first, then with several small deviations to left and right.

2.   35m 6a. Vertically upwards by a line of spits. Traverse slightly left, then direct again to a stance.

3.   50m 6b. A sustained pitch following spits to reach the central garden, with the crux low down.

Either abseil off or continue by the upper 5 pitches of Bucce d'Arancia.

Starting 30m right of the corner of Banano, directly below the central garden is:

Bucce d'Arancia   300m HVS 4c
Lana & Mantoan 4/78

1.   30m 4c. Climb the grey wall towards a small roof, avoid this to the left, and climb up to a good ledge and trees.

2.   30m 4c. Leftwards to a slab with a thin, discontinuous crack line. Follow this, and the corner above to exit rightwards onto a second good ledge.

A harder variation pitch (**Grand Miel** 6a), goes more or less direct, then slightly rightwards from the first stance, continuing up to and avoiding a small roof on its left, before taking a larger one on the left side to join the second stance of Gatta.

3.   30m. Up a little, then traverse easily rightwards by a ramp for about 10m. Directly upwards by a vague rib to stance.

Or, 20m 5a. Go up a little higher and take a diagonal rightwards line to the same stance - the second and final variation pitch of Grand Miel.

4.   30m 4a. Follow a small pillar, avoiding a small roof on its left to reach the central garden.

5.   30m 4b. Cross the garden to reach the base of a good corner/

chimney further right. Follow this enjoyably to the right-hand garden.

6.　30m 4c. Walk back to the wall at the centre of the garden. Up this, make a 2m traverse right to the foot of a corner and climb it.

7.　40m 4a. Up a few metres, diagonally right, then direct again before a final traverse right to vegetation and a stance.

8.　40m 4b. Direct for a few metres, then diagonally leftwards to a good crack which leads to the penultimate stance.

9.　40m. Easy slabs to the top.

Jaccod　300m HVS 5a

　Jaccod & Sestagalli '79

Start as for Diedro below the right-hand garden.

1.　40m 5a. An awkward start leads to open wall climbing before easier moves rightward at 25m lead to a stance.

　(Patata Bollente goes off diagonally leftwards to reach the right-hand garden by 2 pitches of 5b, 5a. Abseil off.)

2.　50m 4b. Diagonally rightwards to a hollow, followed by a flared corner.

3.　25m 5a. Follow a series of thin vertical cracks then traverse right to a stance.

4.　50m 5a. More or less direct to the right end of the right-hand garden.

5.　30m 4c. Follow an open corner diagonally rightwards. Overcome a roof to reach a ledge and trees.

6/7/8.　105m. The climbing becomes progressively easier towards the summit, (maximum 4b).

Diedro　130/300m E1 5b

　Lorenzo et al '77

Probably the best of the older classics, with a superb third pitch up the obvious arched diedre below the right-hand garden, reached by a long traverse from the right. As the gully forming the lower part of the diedre is loose and vegetated, the climb starts just above a dry stone wall some way to the right - 'Diedro' and 'Jaccod' painted on the rock.

1.　25m 5a. Climb more or less directly up the wall to the first stance of 'Poppy' - a route without pegs or bolts, and no longer climbed.

2.　40m 4c. Follow the obvious leftward traverse line - 2 pegs, poor protection. Belay below the corner on pegs, then move up to a higher tree belay before starting the next pitch.

3.　30m 5b. Avoid the repulsive lower section of the corner either by bridging, or thin slab climbing to the left, then hand-traverse left to gain the upper corner. Udge awkwardly up this (crux) and make another hand-traverse left to belay.

4.   35m 5b. Move back right to gain the foot of a smooth rib. Climb this delicately on crystals, then make a long traverse right to cross an overlap. A superb airy pitch.

From here either: (a) Make 3 abseils to the ground. 1)25m. Straight down below the overlap to the stance of Free Volleze. 2)50m. Diagonally right to the first stance of Diedro. 3)To the ground. (To climb **Free Volleze**, abseil straight back to the second stance of Diedro.)

Or: (b) Climb 2 pitches of 30m (4b) and 20m (5a) to reach the right-hand garden. Walk to the left of this and follow cracks and slabs to the summit by another 3 pitches of 4a/b.

Free Volleze 50m E1 5b
Two variant pitches on Diedro give excellent climbing only slightly less fine than the original.

1.   30m 5a. Move right from the second stance of Diedro to gain a rib. Climb this delicately, passing several overlaps.

2.   20m 5b. The curving diedre to the 4th stance of Diedro.

A direct start to Free Volleze is **Maga Mago** (2 pitches of 4c and 5a), and **Free Joint** (50m 5c, 5a) takes a line between Diedro and Free Volleze. Further right are **Il Paradiso Puo Attendere** (30m 5c), and the 3 pitches of **Sghos** (6a, 6a, 5a) - a shiny strip of glacier polish on the extreme right of the cliff.

MACHABY - The Subsidiary Cliffs

THE PARETINA
This short steep wall lies near the foot of the approach path to the main cliff, and is easily identified by its quarried appearance and the cable running diagonally above it. Near vertical and with small flat finger holds, its single pitch climbs are in sharp contrast to those above. They are, from left to right:

U.S.L.   20m 6a.

Scarface   25m E2 5c.

Macbeth   25m E1 5b.

Via di Sotto   25m Severe 4b. (left-hand finish)

Via di Sotto   25m HVS 5a. (right-hand finish)

Tan Dzen   25m HVS 5a.

Aqualung 20m HVS 5b.

Bagno Schiuma 15m HVS 5a.

GRUVIERA

From the parking area below the main cliff, walk or drive 100m towards Verres and a lane goes off to the right. Go up this for a short way to where it forks at a white house (drinking water fountain opposite). Take the right fork, and just after this a track leads through vines to the cliffs. These are more extensive than they appear, and consist of a number of steep buttresses and arêtes with something of the feel of a mini-Tremadoc.

The first obvious buttress has an eroded dyke running right up its centre. Riddled with holes it bears some resemblance to a gruyere cheese - thus the name. All the climbs on this buttress are superb, not least the line of the dyke itself. This is:

Topo Pazzo (Mad Mouse) 80m VS 4c

A superb VS, once only moderately protected, it has been recently equipped with spits. Follow the obvious line in 2 pitches: 1) 45m 4b. 2) 35m 4c to ledge and tree. Abseil off.

The line of bolts close to the right arête is: **Paralisi** 80m E2 5b, 5c (to tree of T. Pazzo).

Just left of Topo Pazzo, and more or less following the arête past a roof on the first pitch, then continuing as for Spigolo, is **Spigolo Pazzo** 80m E2 5b, 5b/c. The face further left is taken by the ineptly named:

Spigolo 80m E2 5c

1. 35m 5b. A boulder problem start leads to a break. Climb the wall by diagonal cracks and overlaps to belay beneath an open corner groove.

2. 30m 5c. Bridge up the groove and past a small roof, before a hard move left leads to an overhang. Over this and up to a stance level with that of Topo Pazzo, (as for Spigolo Pazzo).

Left again is:

Esalibur 50m E1 5b

Another superb pitch giving a harder variant start to Spigolo.

1. 35m 5b. Either make a 6a move to leave the ground, or more sensibly start further left. Steep climbing leads over and around several bulges to exhilarating airy climbing up the fin forming the left wall of the corner of Spigolo.

Left is a stone wall and vines. The impending buttress to the left again contain three hard climbs and an E1.

Due to past damage to vines the access situation regarding these climbs is very delicate, and climbers should verify the latest situation before approaching these routes. It cannot be emphasized too strongly that more damage to vines could result in complete ban on climbing at Gruviera.

These one pitch routes are from left to right:

Transea   E6 6c.

Golgota   E4 6b.

Blade Runner   E3 6a.

Crack   E1 5b.
   Traverse right at the top to belay as for Spigolo - to finish as for pitch 2 of that route, or abseil off.

   Moving back to the right from The Topo Pazzo Buttress the cliffs disappear behind vegetation. Pushing your way through this you come to an obvious, rather vegetated yellow diedre, **Diedro Ribaldone** 80m 5a, 6a). The next corner to the left gives a good HVS:

Diedro Bianco   40m HVS 5a
The rock deteriorates above, so abseil off, or continue by another pitch of mostly 4a/b, with a 5a move to start.

   The line of bolts to the left is: **Dalle du Roi** 6b.

   Dimensione Magica, 80m 4c, 6b, breaks out rightwards from low down on the first pitch of Diedro Bianco to belay near the arête. The second pitch takes the steep wall direct. Also to the right of Diedro Bianco is **Triller** 6b.

THE PILASTRO LOMASTI

This is the clean-looking rock-tower high above Machaby. On closer acquaintance the rock is said to be less solid than it looks. It bears one 7 pitch route, **Via Del 94** - 200m with several pitches of 5b and one of 5c. Previously protected by poor pegs, it has recently been re-equipped with bolts. Another 5 pitch route (3 of which are 6b) has been added, but whether either are worth the 45 minute approach walk from the hamlet of Machaby is unknown.

BISTECCA AREA

Although very close to Machaby this newly developed area is best approached from the south. After Pont St. Martin the N26 passes through Donnas, just after which a small road goes off to the right - signposted 'Bard'. The 25m high flake of Bistecca (Beefsteak), lies just along this on the right. Routes names are painted below.

On the flake itself are:

J.S.   5a.

Adrenaline   5b.

Pane per il Ghiro   5c.

On the wall to the left:

Delirium Tremens

Stati di Allucinazione

Volpini Volanti   5c.

Two hundred metres along the road near a wooden cross are:

Les Freres   5b.

Pas de Problem   5a.

  With development continuing, this list is far from complete.

VALLE DELL'ORCO

Access, Camping, etc.

A line drawn from Chamonix to Turin passes through the Gran Paradiso National Park; find the midpoint of this line and you find Orco. Depending on whether you are approaching from the north (Aosta), or from the south (Turin), take the appropriate turning for Cuorgne off the Aosta-Turin autostrada, and continue on via Pont Canavese and Locana to Noasca. (N.B. On some maps the valley is known as the Valle di Locana.) Being less than 50 miles from Turin, Ceresole and its artificial lake is popular with weekending Torinese. On Saturdays they stream in, and on Sunday afternoons begin their lemming-like homeward rush, turning the normally quiet narrow road into something resembling Monza.

As part of the Gran Paradiso National Park, rough camping is definitely *vietato*, and the rule is strictly enforced by the local police. Most climbers tend to stay at the convenient Sport-Fishing campsite opposite the foot of Sergent, which is well run and reasonably cheap, although there are several other large sites along the main road, as well as smaller, quieter sites alongside the river beyond Ceresole. Both Ceresole and Noasca have shops for basic provisions, but the former offers more in the way of Pizzerias, bars and restaurants, as well as a tourist information centre and a shop with a limited range of climbing equipment (to the right of the restaurant Lo Stambucco).

Introduction

From Pont Canavese onwards, glacier smoothed rock litters the hillside above the narrowing road, although the real prizes are reserved for the five or six twisting miles between Noasca and Ceresole Reale. Here two enormous two hundred metre high masses of granitoid gneiss dominate the south-facing side of the valley. As their early development dates from the '70's, when the image of Yosemite ruled the climbing world, it is not surprising that they were viewed as smaller relatives of El Capitan and dubbed El

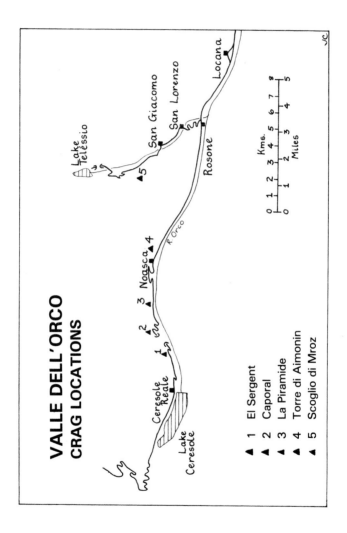

VALLE DELL'ORCO
CRAG LOCATIONS

▲ 1 El Sergent
▲ 2 Caporal
▲ 3 La Piramide
▲ 4 Torre di Aimonin
▲ 5 Scoglio di Mroz

Sergent and Caporal. With the addition of several smaller or less well-developed crags the valley now offers almost the whole spectrum of climbing - bouldering, short hard cracks and slabs, big-wall aid and mixed routes, and long classic free climbs. The scope for new routes is practically unlimited, particularly as the valley does not suffer (?) from Mello's aversion to bolts. However, despite its inclusion in several glossy Italian 'Hard-Rocks', the area is still an unknown quantity even to many Italians, and for the peripatetic 'Brit' it offers some of the best granite climbing outside the U.S.A. Almost in the shadow of the 4,000m Gran Paradiso, and itself at a height of between 1,000m (Noasca), and 1,600m (Ceresole), the valley gets its share of mountain weather, but compares favourably with areas such as Handegg or Chamonix, and the predominantly south facing cliffs dry quickly after rain. Most routes have in-situ protection, but an assortment of nuts and Friends should usually be carried, particularly on the longer climbs.

Guidebooks and Maps
Arrampicate in Valle dell'Orco by Oviglia and Mochino. Pub. Melograno 1987. (Beware the grades - to say they are harsh is an understatement.)

Various maps are available to the Parco Nazionale Gran Paradiso.

Bouldering Minor Crags
The area of boulders opposite the campsite offers numerous problems (although some of the most famous ones have been quarried away). A few metres right of the blue pool is a group of large boulders; on the right side of the right-hand boulder is the **Fissure du Panetton** (20m 6a), a hand-tearing jamming problem freed by Edlinger in June '82. About a hundred metres along the road towards Ceresole is a large boulder forming the left wall of a ruined building. The crack on the left face of this is the famous **Fessura Kosterlitz** (5b). Scotsman Mike Kosterlitz and Gian Piero Motti were the leading activists of the first wave of Orco's development, and it was several years before this crack received a second ascent. Even today it remains a test-piece. Behind this is probably the most popular bouldering area, (note the painted climber on one boulder).

But the jam-crack to end them all is the stunningly photogenic lightning flash of **Sitting Bull** (30m 6b. Manolo '82) on the Parete Blanchetti. Entering the outskirts of Ceresole the Grand Hotel is

25

obvious on the left. On the opposite side of the road are some water-streaked mini-Etive slabs. The Parete is the small crag above and left of these; crag and route are clearly visible from the car park of the Grand Hotel. The track opposite the Bar Blanchetti leads to a path between new apartments. Cross a meadow and follow the path up a wet gully to a summer dwelling on the crest of a rise. The crag lies diagonally up the hillside behind some trees which partially screen it from here. Twenty metres right of this is another crack (5b), with 2 unclimbed corners further right offering the possibility of very hard new routes.

Also worthy of mention is 'Totem Bianco', on the Parete del Disertore across the river behind the campsite. High upon the right-hand side of the face stands a solitary dead pine tree - the Totem Bianco - and the obvious leftward arching flake crack below this provides the fine crux pitch. Freed by Edlinger in '82 at 6b, the remaining pitches are unfortunately of a much easier VS standard.

EL SERGENT

With its ease of access, quick drying southerly aspect and wide variety of length, type and grade of climbing, Sergent is the most popular of the Orco crags.

From the Sport-Fishing campsite opposite, its main features are clearly visible above the trees. The extreme left is a sweep of easy angled slabs guarded below by steep, dark walls, the slabs becoming steeper and more continuous where they join the central wall. It is on this 100m wide face between here and the obvious rock tower of the 'Lost Arrow' that most of the routes are to be found. Just left of the Arrow, the thin line running diagonally leftwards is the man-eating offwidth of Disperazione. The foot of the cliff dips to its lowest point on the extreme right, and Locatelli takes the evident crack/chimney system up the pillar to the left of this.

Approach & Descent

From the blue pool opposite the campsite, zig-zag steeply up through boulders then bear right following a path to the foot of the main face. 20 minutes.

Unless otherwise indicated, descents are by abseil. The routes are described from right to left.

Locatelli (or Via della Rampa)   170m E2 5c
Locatelli & Duregon 6/74 (Direct finish Morello & Motti 6/74)

El Sergent

1 - Diedro Mistero
2 - Abseil ledge abow
   Central Wall
3 - Disperazione
4 - Lost Arrow
5 - Locatelli

From the Lost Arrow follow a beaten path rightwards, descending steeply to the base of an obvious corner, left of a huge chimney.

1. 30m 5b. The steep crack and detached flake to ledge and blocks.

2. 25m 4b. More flakes lead left then straight up to a pine tree.

3. 35m 4b. Easy slabs leftwards to small yellow corner. Up this and the roof above on its left. Tree belay above.

4. Walk across the terrace to the foot of an obvious crack/ chimney system.

5. 35m 5c. Hard moves on slightly friable rock lead to an easy slab inside the chimney. A unique and atmospheric pitch.

6. 10m. Speleological. Up easily leftwards to cave. Remove all bandoliers, slings, etc., and push these through the cannon hole above before squirming after. (The more corpulent or claustrophobic can avoid this on the outside - harder and less fun.)

From here either; make a strenuous pull up to the right to gain a large ledge. Walk off right to pine trees and make two exciting 40m abseils, and one short one to regain the foot of the route. (The crack and overhang above the pine trees gives a pleasant 15m VS pitch.)

Or:

7. 20m AO 4c. (6b free?) Move up to where the chimney closes, and using an in-situ peg and small wire for aid, pull over the roof above on its left. Thrutch up the continuation crack.

8. 15m 5b. After an awkward move, more easily up the corner to exit via a short wall onto a terrace. Walk right to a pine tree, from where a 35m free abseil leads to the ledge described above.

N.B. The in-situ aid on pitch 7 was said to be in a dangerous condition in August '86.

Some metres down to the right of Locatelli is **Elisir d'Incastro** 60m 5c/6a. Said to be one of the finest cracks in the valley and with a trying crux to pass the roof at the top of the first pitch.

The Central Wall is broken by a roughly horizontal ledge at approx. 50m and with the exception of Disperazione and the Nicchia delle Torture/Cannabis combination, all the climbs normally finish at abseil points on this ledge. However, almost all of the routes can be combined with the upper pitches of these two climbs.

Note: The brutal roof crack above the ledge is taken by **Incastro Amaro** 6c. Bernardi '82.

Fessura della Disperazione   150m E10 5b

  Galante, Lenzi, Bonelli 5/74

1.   30m 5a. From a large block left of the Lost Arrow follow the obvious diagonal crack leftwards (often making good use of the right foot!) to a hanging stance on small nuts below the horizontal section.

2.   25m 5b. Continue leftwards until the crack becomes vertical. The next 8m of offwidth are completely unprotected.

3.   25m 5a. Follow the crack, first vertically, then more easily leftwards to a good ledge.

4.   25m 4c. The corner above, then a short ramp leftwards to another good ledge below the chimney clearly visible from below, (Camino Bernardi).

5.   35m 5b. Climb the chimney to a stance beneath a jammed block.

6.   10m 4b. Climb the arête to the left and exit over a block to a grassy terrace.

  From here either continue by another 5 easy pitches to the summit, or (more usual) traverse left (west), descending slightly by slabs and ledges towards a dry pine tree easily visible from the last stance. After some blocks, a slanting crack leads down to another pine. Make a 40m abseil from this trending slightly leftwards, then another of 40m from spikes in a deep horizontal crack. Go slightly right to a flake with slings and make a third 40m abseil to the foot of the wall.

  Twenty metres left of the start of Disperazione, starting up a corner on the right side of a block, is the S shaped jam-crack of:

Incastro Mania   30m E1 5b (abseil off dubious tat).

  Left of this is the faint crack line of **Cannabis** (freed in late '86 at 6c), and left again the grassy ramp and zig-zag crack of:

Nicchia delle Torture   70m E2 5c (140m E4 6b when combined with upper pitches of Cannabis).

  Meneghin & Crotti 10/77 (Galante & Grassi 10/73)

1.   35m 4c. Follow a ramp and disintegrating earth ledges leftwards past the belay chains of 'Danza in Trance' to peg belay below corner.

2.   35m 5c. A perfect jam-crack leads to an awkward and poorly protected traverse right. Hide in the niche before taking the crack in the roof and its easier continuation. Up to the large ledge and abseil off, or continue up Cannabis;

3.   25m 4c. Move right and up a corner to a stance on the terrace

below the chimney of Camino Bernardi.

4. 35m 6b. The steep crack left of the chimney, (several in-situ pegs).

5. 10m 4b. This pitch and descent as for pitch 6 of Disperazione.

The line of bolts to the left is: **Danza in Trance** 25m E3/4 6b. (Mochino 6/86).

Left of this is a diagonal right to left crack parallel with the ramp of Torture. Starting left of the foot of this is:

Paperinik Colpisce Ancora 35m E3 5c
   Mola '83

Hard unproteccted moves lead to the crack, followed by more poorly protected slab climbing up to the first stance of Torture.

High up to the left is an eye-catching leftward curving arch, giving the crux pitch of:

Diedro del Mistero E2 5c
   Galante et al 5/74

(A historic breakthrough. Bonelli's free ascent in 1978 was the first pitch of hand-jamming to be recorded in all of Italy!)

Scramble up to two trees at foot of a ramp leading R.

1. 35m 5b. Easily up the ramp to a peg/bolt, left to a crack and follow this to the base of the diedre/arch.

2. 25m 5c. Strenuous jamming leads past several pegs to a lay-back exit. Abseil from the ledge above (the original route continued to the right to finish as for Cannabis).

Delirio della Solitudine 50m E3 6b
   Vogler '83.

Starting from the trees of Mistero, the line of bolts leading first left then virtually straight up, is probably the finest slab climb on Sergent, with a particularly trying move to pass the second bolt.

The easier angled slabs to the left are taken by two long, easy slab climbs; **Via delle Placche**, V with a pitch of A1, but mostly IV and III (Lenzi, Vota & Vignazia '73); and **Apparizione de Cristo Verde**, mostly VS but with a move of 5b on the second pitch.

CAPORAL

Partially screened by the boulder field at its foot, the true grandeur of the great bastion of Caporal is only revealed from some way up the approach path. On the right, the huge almost featureless S face (Lo Scudo - The Shield) is breached only by the artificial routes of **Rivoluzione** and **Crazy Horse;** and the majority of routes on

CAPORAL

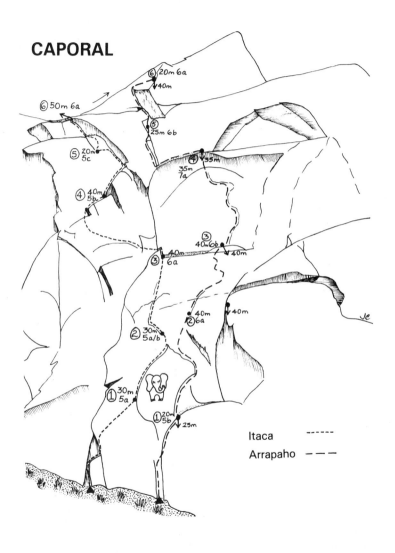

⑥ 20m 6a
↓40m

⑥ 50m 6a

⑤ 25m 6b

⑤ 20m 5c

④ 35m 7a ↓35m

④ 40m 5b

③ 40m 6b ↓40m

③ 40m 6a

② 40m 6a ↓40m

② 30m 5a/b

① 30m 5a

① 20m 5b ↓25m

Itaca - - - - -
Arrapaho — — —

31

Caporal still employ large amounts of aid - the super routes of tomorrow. The only free climbs are to be found on the SW face to the left, although all of these are still often ascended with varying amounts of aid. However, the quality of experience to be enjoyed on these three routes is equal to that found anywhere in Europe or California. The rock is superbly sound and free of vegetation, and the cliff has a feeling of remoteness rarely encountered with such easy access - chamois are often seen from the screes below, and our ascent of the lower part of Itaca was accompanied by the screams of an eagle circling high above us.

The centre of the SW face is characterized by the huge crack-line of Tempi Moderni, and the slabs right of this provide the lower pitches of Itaca/Tempi Moderni and Arrapaho - the latter continuing up the impressive vertical headwall above (Lo Specchio - The Mirror), whereas Itaca/Tempi Moderni avoids this to the left by a series of cracks. At the extreme left, the face is split by the huge impending corner of Diedro Nanchez. All three routes have a fair amount of in-situ protection, but carry a reasonable rack of nuts and Friends - particularly for Itaca and Nanchez.

Approach. From Noasca, the road to Ceresole Reale rises by a series of hairpin bends to a straight section, followed by a second series of hairpins. After the last of these the road enters a gallery. To the right of the gallery mouth is an obvious parking area, with Caporal clearly visible above. Take one of the paths up the steep scree slope towards the S face. The paths come together at some easy slabs which are crossed rightwards. Trend back to the left towards the SW face (keeping another set of slabs on the left). 25 minutes.

Itaca nel Sole/Tempi Moderni 200m E4 6a (E1/2 5c/A1)
Motti & Morelli 6/75, Motti et al 10/72

A stupendous route, and the most sought-after classic in the whole of Orco. If pitch 3 and the final crack of pitch 6 are aided, the overall grade becomes E1 5c; still very worthwhile and probably the most usual form of ascent. Harder climbers may prefer to start with the first 2 pitches of L'Orecchio del Pachiderma (see Arrapaho), although it is a pity to miss the comparatively easy, but very enjoyable climbing of the normal second pitch.

The arête between the S and SW faces overhangs at its foot. Left of this is the obvious chimney of Via dei Camini, and several metres left again is a large square niche below the dominating dierdre of Tempi Moderni. Start on the left of the large blackish block in the centre of the niche (often wet).

1.   20m 5a. Climb up onto the block and traverse right to an impending crack. Up this and the flake above. Stance round to the right - second may need to lead through for a few metres to belay, thus avoiding rope drag on the second pitch.

2.   30m 5a/b. Follow flakes, then the crack on the left to stance and pegs. (The right-hand crack is Arrapaho.) A superb pitch.

3.   40m 6a. Up the crack on the left (pegs), then the thin slab above (many peg-bolts - climb left of these at first to free climb). At the end of the bold-ladder traverse left, then up the edge of the slab to belay on the huge terrace below the great wall of Lo Specchio.

4.   40m 5b. Layback the short corner crack (or the A1 crack just left, 6b free), and continue to large block. Make a long diagonal traverse left over ledges, return right and climb a diedre to belay.

5.   20m 5c. The crack in the wall to the left (several pegs), belay on the ledge above.

6.   50m 6a. Cross a cracked slab obliquely rightwards, and return left to the foot of an obvious overhanging corner/groove (many pegs). Climb this to a strenuous leftward exit. Continue leftwards over easy slabs to belay.

Descent.   Cross easy slabs to the right (east) for 20m to chains above Lo Specchio. Make 2 abseils of 40 and 35m to the chains in the centre of the large terrace, i.e. right of the third stance. A 40m abseil leads diagonally rightwards to a ledge and chains, and another of the same length bears slightly leftwards to the foot of the crack of Pachiderma. Finally a shorter abseil down the first chimney of Camini returns you to the foot of the face.

Arrapaho   180m E6/7/7a
  Marco Pedrini '86

From the parking space, a curving crack in the shape of an ear is clearly visible below the slab of Itaca. This is the Orecchio del Pachiderma - the Elephants Ear. With the creation of two hard slab pitches, Pedrini linked this to the previously aided 4th pitch of Itaca up the centre of Lo Specchio (first placing protection bolts by abseil). Two more very hard pitches up the left-hand side of the final headwall completed the most dramatic and sustained climb in Orco. In 1986 some of the bolt hangers had been removed from pitch 4, though it is said to be possible to protect it with R.P.s.

  N.B. L'Orecchio del Pachiderma is unusual in that it lacks in-situ protection - carry Friends 2 to 4. It also makes a fine climb in its own right (E2 5c - abseil off above the crack).

  Start at the foot of the chimney of 'Camini'.

1.   20m 5b. Climb the crack in the left wail of the chimney, then traverse right to belay below the rightward slanting crack of the Orecchio.

2.   40m 6a. Climb the crack, then more directly up a slab and flake.

3.   40m 6b. The smooth slab above, first trending right, then back left to a stance on the large terrace.

4.   35m 7a. The thin crack in the searing reddish wall. Belay on the good ledge above.

5.   25m 6b. From the left end of the ledge, the steep crack becomes a difficult offwidth - thankfully with bolts.

6.   20m 6a. Continue in the same line to the top.

   Descend as for Itaca/Tempi Moderni.

Diedro Nanchez   175m E2 5c
   Galante, Motti, Bonelli et al 10/74

Another superlative route - very sustained, yet never excessively difficult, giving surprisingly varied climbing. Being a natural watercourse it is unfortunately often wet, and at least a week of dry weather is needed to ensure completely dry conditions - September and October are often favourable.

   From the start of Itaca continue steeply for another 200m up the gully below the SW face, until just below its top. Nanchez takes the obvious leftward trending diedre with a huge flake on its left wall at about 30m. To the left and below this, an undercut ramp runs from right to left.

1.   30m 5c. Make a strenuous pull onto the ramp, and move right until a crack leads easily to a good ledge and tree.

2.   45m 5b. Enjoyable laybacking leads to a roof; pass this on its left to reach a good crack leading to a stance with peg and spike belays.

3.   40m 5b. After a chimney, an easy layback leads to a steeper crack and a difficult exit onto a ledge - beware large loose block!

4.   40m 5c. Move awkwardly rightwards around blocks, returning leftwards to enter a fantastic diedre. Up this by an enjoyable combination of laybacking and wide bridging, before a final section of hard jamming up the crack splitting the huge jammed flake above. A better pitch would be hard to find.

5.   20m 5b. (40m in total) Move up the corner below the final roof, and make a series of peculiar moves to gain a ledge on the left (2 very welcome pegs). Continue along the ledge and the subsequent slab to the end of the rock. It is difficult to belay here, so move up 20m over grass to a peg belay.

Descent. Scramble upwards away from the edge of the cliff, then bear right (facing in) to eventually gain the abseil descent as for Itaca. Alternatively, scramble back from the face as above, then follow a worn path diagonally leftwards over earth and rock ledges for about 80m to where a cairned path returns you to the foot of Caporal.

N.B. The above pitches are longer than those given in the old guidebook, and are described as I climbed them in August 1984. With the large number of pegs in-situ it would be easy to split the route into shorter pitches if so desired.

LA PIRAMIDE

Approaching from Noasca, after the first set of hairpin bends the road flattens out. Piramide is the obvious 100m high triangular slab just above the right-hand side of the road. Immediately after this the road passes through a narrow gap blasted through an enormous boulder, park before this on the left. Another huge boulder lies below the foot of the face, which is split by two cracks forming an extended 'V'. **Fessura per P.A.** takes the right-hand of these, whereas **Cacao** and **Budino** are to be found on the smooth east face around to the right. Walk easily across meadows and scramble up to a ledge behind the huge boulder (good for leaving sacs).

Descent. For P.A. and Legolas, walk back through the trees following a path rightwards to the top of a short wall above a grassy gully. Make a 10m abseil from a tree and continue down the gully to a grassy terrace above a subsidiary slab. Walk along this and so return to the foot of the routes.

Fessura per P.A. 120m H.Severe 4b
  Motti (solo) 6/74
Start at the foot of the crack below the junction of the 'V', behind the huge block.
1.   40m 4b. The undercut start to the crack is probably the hardest move of the climb. Continue more easily by good jamming, taking the right fork where the crack splits, to a stance at 2 horizontal cracks.
2.   40m. Continue easily but enjoyably, in the same line.
3.   40m 4a. Traverse left for a few metres to a crack with a jammed block. Climb this and the easy slabs above.

Legolas .... Humm Tutta Libera   130m VS 4c
  Bonelli & Demichela 6/74
A good first pitch followed by a wandering line across the slabs right of P.A. Perhaps best used either as an alternative start to P.A. or as a short 2 pitch route to the first stance of that route, and abseil off. Start 10m left of the huge boulder, beneath a short crack by a group of blocks.
1. 30m 4c. Climb the crack and continue more or less direct until a diagonal traverse rightwards leads to a small ledge just to the left of the left-hand branch of the 'V'.
2. 20m. Traverse right crossing the 2 cracks, and continue traversing, descending slightly, to a stance on the rounded arête.
  Another 80m (hardest moves 4b) first moving generally rightwards to a grassy ledge, and then moving back left, lead to the top. (2 to 4 pitches as desired.)

Cacao   80m E3 5c A0 (E5 6b) Free
  Ogliengo & Dusi 6/81
From the huge block below P.A. walk right along the grassy terrace (the reverse of the descent) to a point above the second set of lower slabs where a leaning corner crack (mossy above) abuts the upper slab.
1. 35m 5c. Up diagonally rightwards to a peg at 6m, move up to 2 bolts and make a hard horizontal traverse rightwards (peg) to a scoop. Continue diagonally right to a rib and then direct past several bolts to gain a ledge (awkward). Peg/bolt belay.
2. 50m 5b/c. (Serious). A short holdless vertical step guards the upper slab. Either pass this with the aid of the wobbly bolt, or move 2m right and free climb at 6b. The next bolt is the last protection for almost 10m - follow the faint scooped water-streak up the slab above (delicate and sustained 5a/b) passing 2 more bolts with a harder section below the last of these. Go diagonally right to tree belays.

Budino alla Fragolo   20m E3 6a
  Zanone '85
Some metres right of the start of Cacao is a clean section of slab with an obvious step at about 5m. Start below this (bolts).
1. 20m 6a. Climb up and then diagonally rightward to the step. Make a thin move to attain this, and continue direct to another hard section before moving left to a stance.

La Piramide

Abseil off or move left to the stance of Cacao and continue up pitch 2 of this.

Note: The large vertical face left of Piramide is Il Cubo, with its classic line 'Cochise'. Despite its fine appearance, the rock is poor and Cochise a poorly protected, serious climb.

TORRE DI AIMONIN

Above and right of Noasca, the tower is best viewed when the morning light begins to reveal the architecture of its arêtes and corners. The left arête is taken by Spigolo, whereas Pesce d'Aprile takes a wandering rightward line from the foot of this to the obvious dierdre in the centre of the face. La Casa degli Specchi breaks through the roofs guarding the foot of the crag, before crossing Pesce at the short layback flake to eventually take the stunning crackline in the top wall between this and Spigolo (originally Manolo's direct finish to the latter). Right of the lower roofs a large rock pillar abuts the face, 'Diedro' HVS, takes the huge corner on the left of this, (4 worthwhile pitches, plus 1 of trees, grass and earth to finish).

Facing SW, Aimonin provides pleasantly shady morning climbing during hot weather, or sunny afternoons and evenings in spring and autumn.

Approach and Descent
The old approach from the cemetery was less than easy to find or follow, but the recently waymarked path (red spots) allows the foot of the crag to be attained in a comfortable 20 minutes. Park in the square at Noasca, and cross the road to the church opposite. Pass this on the right and follow the path that leads first left behind buildings and then rightwards across the hillside to the crag. The descent is similarly marked; follow the path horizontally right across the top of the crag and down the other side, returning beneath the foot of the crag.

Pesce d'Aprile (April Fool) 170m HVS 5a
  Mike Kosterlitz, Motti et al 3/73
Start at a small cave on the extreme left of the cliff.
1. 20m. Easily up just left of the arête to a large ledge. Belay to the right below a corner.
2. 40m 4a. Climb the right wall of the corner, then traverse easily right for 20m to a large flake-crack. Up this to belay on right.

3.   40m 4c. The short layback flake on the right, followed by more rightward traversing over easy slabs to the foot of the diedre visible from below.

4.   25m 5a. The superb diedre.

5.   20m 4b. Move up to the roof and go through this to the right. Continue diagonally rightwards to a tree belay.

6.   25m 4b. Up to a niche and tree, and take the fine jam crack to a sandy finish.

Spigolo   145m E1 5b
   Re & Bonino 5/73

1.   35m. From the cave of Pesce d'Aprile follow easy grassy corners and arêtes, until a groove leads to a ledge and peg belays.

2.   25m 4c/5a. The steep crack in the yellow wall on the left (pegs) leads back to the arête on the right. Follow an easy slab to a peg belay.

3.   35m 5b. Go slightly right to the obvious overhang and take this by the thin crack (pegs), or by the jam crack further right at the same standard (Friend 3). Move up to the cave and swing enjoyably out over the lip on the right. Follow cracks to a stance at the ledge on the left, taking care with perched blocks.

4.   50m 5a. Up the crack behind the stance (pegs), then more easily by cracks and grooves trending rightwards to finish up an easy but exposed and unprotected slab, (or more easily up a crack to the right). Nut and thread belays on the ledge above. It is possible to split this pitch below the final slab.

Descent.   A waymarked path (red spots) leads horizontally right across the top of the crag, and down the other side.

La Casa degli Specchi (The House of Mirrors)   210m E4 6a
   Caneparo & Mochino '83

Start on the jumble of the huge boulders below the large horizontal roof at 20m, between Spigolo on the left, and the great corner of Diedro to the right. the first 2 and last 2 pitches are particularly fine, although the easier pitches between tend to break the continuity. In August '86 the route had had few ascents, and the first pitch was a little friable and lichenous.

1.   25m 6a. Make an awkward step off the blocks to gain a ramp, and zig-zag across the wall to the corner on the right. This is hard both to start and continue - belay under the roof.

2.   20m 5a. Traverse left under the roof, and pull around the end of this. Pass the 2 pegs of the original stance to a better stance with nut belays a few metres higher.

TORRE DI AIMONIN

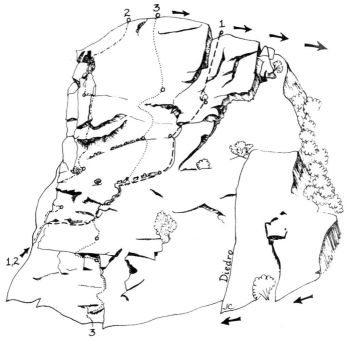

```
---- · 1    Pesce d'Aprile
-·-·-·-. 2    Spigolo
············ 3    La Casa degli Specchi
```

3.   40m 4b. Follow a ramp diagonally left to a ledge, then follow P' d'Aprile back right to a stance.

4.   25m 4c. Layback the flake on the right (as for P' d'Aprile pitch 3) and go up and slightly left to a stance just below and left of the diedre of P' d'Aprile - peg and nuts.

5.   25m 4c. Slabs trend generally leftwards to an obvious stance below and right of the cave of Spigolo.

6.   30m 5a. Take the crack above the stance, then follow flakes up left to near the right edge of the cave. Pull up and return delicately right by a diagonal ramp before moving up to a ledge with 2 pegs. (This last section is virtually unprotected and needs a steady second.)

7.   45m 6a. Move up to and climb the finger crack splitting the headwall above. Several pegs. Sustained, brilliant climbing.

SCOGLIO DI MROZ

Named in memory of Andrez Mroz who died on the Aiguille Noire at the time of the first explorations here, this impressive granite spire stands high above the Valle Piantonetto. Its remoteness and consequent length of access will discourage many; but to others, these very factors, combined with its excellent climbing, a drive up a beautiful and picturesque alpine valley, and a unique 'tunnel' approach, are the ingredients for a perfect climbing day.

Approach
From the campsite opposite Sergent, drive 9 miles back towards Pont Canavese, turn very sharply left for the Valle di Piantonetto which is signposted just before entering the village of Rosone. From the opposite direction the turning lies 3 miles after Locana. Follow the steep winding road through the hamlet of San Lorenzo (bar) and pass under the first cable-car wires (which lead up to a dam). After about 4 miles of superb rock scenery (all virtually undeveloped!), the road becomes a track; shortly another track leads steeply up to the station for the second cableway. Scoglio di Mroz is the clean rock spire visible above the cable station. Either park here, or continue steeply up to the cable station.

A vague path starts right of the station and leads steeply up grassy, wooded slopes, followed by large scree right of the stream bed. The path becomes blocked by a mass of huge boulders, but fortunately a natural tunnel leads through them. Follow the tunnel for some 25m (!) and scramble out the other end. A stick is

SCOGLIO DI MROZ

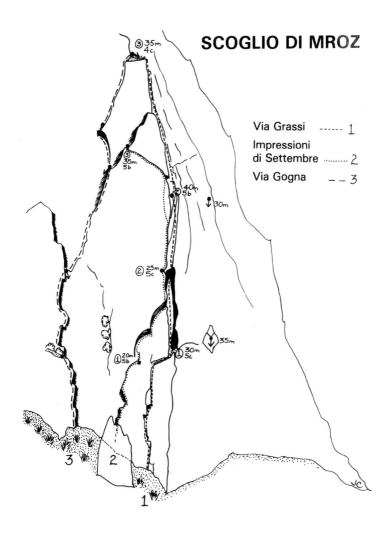

Via Grassi ----- 1

Impressioni
di Settembre 2

Via Gogna -- 3

usually placed in a prominent position at this exit, as it can be difficult to locate on return. It is advisable that at least one member of
the party is equipped with a headtorch for this purpose, an alternative to the tunnel would be very hard to find, and the path is
generally more difficult to follow in descent. Continue straight up,
then bear left under a sub-cliff before returning to the right above
this. Aiming for the right arête of the tower, scramble up grassy
ledges to reach this, and thus the foot of the routes.

1 hour (perhaps longer in the raspberry and bilberry season).

Via Grassi   105m E2 5c (E1 5b/A0)
   Grassi & Griseri 5/74
After the first moves, the climbing is enjoyably sustained E1 in
superb positions, following cracks to the right of the arête
between the E and S faces of a semi-detached tower (La Torre
Staccata) which forms the lower half of this side of the spire. The
hard move to enter the first crack is at least 5c for the short, but an
in-situ peg provides moral (or other forms of) support. Well
protected by medium and large nuts, and a few in-situ pegs.
   Start below the flake crack just left of the arête.
1.   30m 5c. The thin crack leads to the flake, at the top of this
traverse around the arête to the right to belay in a cave at the foot
of a chimney.
2.   40m 5b. Climb the chimney and pull over the roof onto a
steep slab. Follow twin cracks right of the continuation of the
chimney, to a peg belay.
3.   35m 4c. Continue up the crack and gain a ledge. Either (a) go
to the back of this and climb the slightly muddy crack before
swinging out left onto the short impending wall; or (b) move
almost immediately left onto the wall and climb this strenuously on
good holds. Both ways lead to a large ledge at the top of the Torre
Staccata.
   The original route reached the top of Mroz by another 3 pitches
of 4c and A1, but the rock is more broken and vegetated above
and it is better to abseil from here and climb one of the other routes
described below.
Descent.   3 abseils. 1) 35m. From a block on the edge of the
ledge diagonally right down slabs on the right of the route
ascended, to a niche with 2 pegs. 2) 30m. To a large block below
and left. 3) 35m. To the ground.

Impressioni di Settembre   80m E3 5c
   Oviglia, Caneparo & Mochino 9/83

A worthy, but much harder partner to the above. The climbing is more strenuous and sustained, and less well protected, with the final hand-traverse in a spectacular position.

Start by scrambling up onto the large block below the layback flake some metres left of the Grassi route.

1.   20m 5b. The strenuous flake leads to a more delicate traverse to a stance on the right.

2.   25m 5c. Continue in the same line with a difficult hand-change under the small roof. Move up the crack above to belay on the arête (just left of the Grassi).

3.   35m 5b. Up the crack and move onto and around the arête to the left. Superbly exposed unprotected slab climbing (at about 4b), leads to a ledge on the arête. The diagonal crack leading leftwards across the slightly undercut wall gives strenuous, but well protected jamming. Belay on a ledge that continues right behind the detached flake that forms the wall!

Climb down a few metres to the left to join the Gogna route -exposed, but easier than it looks, and a back rope can be rigged. From here either (a) continue up the Gogna route by 2 20m pitches of A1 and 4c (6a free?) to reach the top of the Torre Staccata; or (b) make a 10m abseil to the ledge visible below, and another of 40m to the foot of the Gogna route.

The Via Gogna (or 'Torre Staccata') reaches this point in 3 pitches of 4c, 5a, 4b, starting up a corner below trees and continuing by means of huge, hollow flakes.

LA VALLE SUSA

Running roughly westwards from Turin to the ancient Roman garrison town of Susa and the ski resorts of Sauze d'Oulx, Sestriere and Bardonecchia beyond; the Susa Valley is one of the most important lines of communication between France and Italy. But it is the variety of rock types found in the 30 miles between Turin and Susa that makes the area of such interest to the climber. From the serpentines and prasinites of Caprie, through the granite of Borgone, to the marbled limestone of Foresto and Striature Nera, the valley exhibits a geological diversity rarely found in such a compact area.

Add the low altitude of the predominantly south facing cliffs which enables climbing to take place for most of the year, plus their ease of access for the thousands of climbers from Turin and surrounding towns and villages, and it seems remarkable that so little development took place until the 1970's. As elsewhere in Italy, most of the climbs of the 70's relied heavily on aid and it was only with the free-climbing ethic of the 80's (and the use of spits) that the valley became a major climbing centre.

The heavy traffic normally encountered on the main roads through the valley has little or no effect on the cliff environments, and the processions of trucks are really only a problem on the steep climb up from Susa to Bardonecchia. The autostrada under construction will do much to alleviate the latter, but probably at the expense of the former as it is projected to pass very close to Foresto. We should perhaps be grateful that this lower section of motorway is unlikely to be even started for some considerable time.

Camping
The main valley is intensively cultivated and with the exception of Bardonecchia, rough camping is extremely difficult to find. However it may be possible to camp for short periods on hay meadows bordering the minor road of the side-valleys if permission

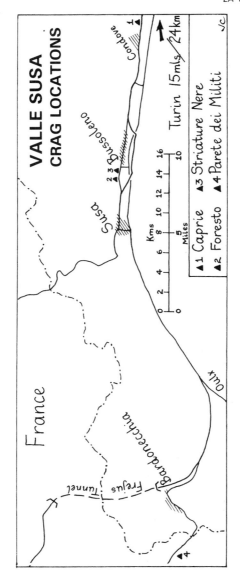

VALLE SUSA CRAG LOCATIONS

France

Condove

Bussoleno

Susa

Oulx

Bardonecchia

Frejus Tunnel

Turin 15mls/24km

Kms
Miles

0 2 4 6 8 10 12 14 16
5 10

▲1 Caprie   ▲3 Striature Nere
▲2 Foresto   ▲4 Parete dei Militi

47

is first sought from the local people. There are campsites at Bussoleno, San Giorio and at the Laghi di Avigliana (signposted from the N25 a few km outside of Turin). It would be possible to base oneself at Bardonecchia, but with the heavy traffic, the driving to and from Foresto, Caprie etc. would be less than enjoyable.

Guidebooks

At the time of writing, no guidebooks exist for either the cliffs of Foresto/Striature Nera, or Bardonecchia. The cliffs of Caprie have been fully documented by one of the area's leading activists, but although the guidebook contains photodiagrams to illustrate most of its 150 routes, it would be very difficult to use without a reasonable understanding of Italian, particularly in view of the difficult access to many of the cliffs.

Arrampicate in Valle Susa - Itinerari a Caprie by Gian Carlo Grassi 1986. Pub. Ghibaudo.

CAPRIE

Caprie is an extensive and complicated group of cliffs behind the village of the same name - easily reached by the main SS24 road about 15 miles from the outskirts of Turin, (or by the SS25 and turning right onto the 24 at Avigliana). Because of their differing aspects climbing is possible throughout the year, although it is uncommon from December to February and as the majority of the crags face south, they are also so hot as to be virtually unclimbable in the height of summer. However, the climbs selected here lie within the gorge (known as the Gola) where the moist air and shade make them particularly suitable for the hotter months, although as the first ascents of two of the routes took place in November and December, they can obviously be enjoyed at other times of the year. The two cliffs of the Pilastro San Marco and the Parete di Eriador lie within sight of each other on opposing sides of the gorge, but the approaches are completely different.

THE PILASTRO SAN MARCO

Rising up from the atmospheric pools and waterfalls of the gorge is the impressive pillar of San Marco, and the powerful line described here is more than equal to its magnificent surroundings. Combined

Pilastro San Marco
1 - Via San Marco
2 - Maga Mago

with a swim or an exploration of the gorge, the approach walk itself makes an enjoyable outing.

Approach

Coming into Caprie there is a good view of the cliffs from the first junction, with the large mass of Rocca Bianca/Nera above and right. Below this is Anticaprie, and the Gola can be seen ahead and slightly left. Turn first left and then sharp right onto the Via Lino Maffiodo which bears sharply right just before it reaches the Piazza San Rocco. Park here.

Walk between the church and the trattoria to a footbridge over the Rio Sessi. Follow this left past a wash-house along a pack-horse trail which rises steeply to the first hairpin bend on the right. Leave this by a path on the left which continues along the river-bank. Follow this, ignoring small paths going down to the river, until you reach a sweet chestnut tree with 8 trunks, and a large boulder left of this in the stream. (Go straight on for a few metres to obtain a good view of the climb and a spectacular waterfall.) Turn sharply right and follow a path up steeply through trees to gain the top of a steep gully. Descend this with the help of friendly trees to reach the foot of the climb (and an excellent pool for swimming). From here an earthy ledge leads up diagonally leftwards to the foot of Via San Marco. 20 minutes from Caprie.
Descent. From the summit slabs cross to the right (facing the rock) to gain the track which returns you to Caprie.

N.B. In view of this it is best either to leave sacs in the car, or hide them at the point where the path breaks off from the track.

Via San Marco   140m E4 6a

Cosson & Vittoni 8/79

On excellent rock, this is one of the best and most sustained Susa routes. Although well protected, the climbing is strenuous and exposed, with the traverse on pitch 4 particularly intimidating for the second. As retreat could mean abseiling into the river (which reaches 2 metres in depth in spring) a degree of commitment is required from both leader and second. Carry a full rack of nuts, Friends 1 to 3, and plenty of quick-draws.

Go easily up earthy ledges to the left to gain a ledge with peg-bolts.

1.   25m 4b. Follow the ramp/crack then traverse left to a terrace at the foot of a fine vertical corner.
2.   25m 5b. Climb this and exit left to a robust tree visible from

below.

3.   40m 6a. Climb easily above the tree to a crack up the vertical wall and follow this to an overhang. Over this to the left, then up the exposed arête forming the most obvious feature of the climb. Follow its edge by sustained climbing (crux) to a good ledge.

4.   30m 5b/c. Easily right to the foot of a perfect diedre. Make a difficult, slightly descending traverse right along an undercut ledge to reach a vertical crack. (The original route took a delicate lower traverse line.) Up the crack and another larger crack (which becomes a flake) to a possible belay. Cross the diedre to the left to an arête and reach a good stance.

5.   20m 4b. Go slightly right and climb the good cracked slab direct. Follow slabs to the summit.

Maga Mago   150m 6a
   Degani & Ogliengo 11/82

Starting from the first stance of San Marco, this is another sustained route which follows a faint vertical crack line and arête to the right of that route. Said to be of similar quality to San Marco, but to need pegs for protection which are not in place.

THE PARETE DI ERIADOR

The routes described here are all on the right-hand of the three pillars which make up the Parete di Eriador - a rounded slab of clean rock with a steep mass of vegetation at its summit. Although only slightly upstream from the Pilastro San Marco, it is not possible to reach the foot of the routes from that cliff, and the only access is by abseil. However, this is very well equipped, and the approach adds to the atmosphere of the climbs. The rock is excellent and the two slab climbs are in sharp contrast to the steep cracks of San Marco, with climbing similar to the gneiss of Machaby - but with better protection. Here I have taken the best pitches from 3 routes, to make 2 excellent slab climbs which follow more logical lines than the originals. Nani di Spirito finds its way up the steeper rock left of the slabs, giving sustained fingery climbing with excellent protection.

Approach

From Turin turn left at the junction coming into Caprie, then right. Where this road swings right into the village, go straight on through a narrow gap in the buildings, heading for the village of

Pero Aldrado. After 2 miles of steep winding road, park in a small square in front of an old church on the left (tap). Walk back the way you have come to a wooden weekend chalet on the opposite side of the road. Pass through the gate, and keeping the building on your left, follow the path upwards through the wood to a clearing with a large whale-backed boulder (and a profusion of small cacti). Pass to the left of the boulder, and continue in this line to where the path crosses a ruined wall in a corner. Descend over rocks through scrubby woodland, finally turning right under an ivied slab - leave sacs here. Crossing a smaller boulder, go down to a group of oak trees with in-situ slings on the edge of the gorge. Two easy abseils lead to the foot of the routes:

(1) 25m. to 2 sets of chains on earth ledge.

(2) 40m. to a tree 10m above spiny vegetation, with a ramp and crack bearing diagonally leftwards past 2 trees. All the routes are described from here. If you wish to look at the bed of the gorge make another short abseil, or climb down.

Nani di Spirito   65m E4 6a
Alpe & Grassi 8/83

1.   30m 6b. Follow the crack and ramp on the left to the second tree. Move diagonally rightwards by a series of flakes (pegs) to a greenish ledge. Up a vertical wall to a flake (bolt and pegs), and move diagonally left to another flake before hard moves lead horizontally left past a bolt. Continue diagonally leftward to rejoin the continuation of the initial crack and ramp. Peg belay.

2.   15m 6a. Steeply rightwards to the stance of Flutti Ipnotici - the second abseil point.

3.   20m. Any line to the top.

Flutti Ipnotici   75m E1 5b
Grassi & Meneghin 11/82

1.   20m 5a. Follow the crack on the left to the first tree. Move right onto the slab and make an awkward step up. Follow a flake for a few metres, then go right to 2 pegbolts. Up to the right, then left to the start of a flake leading to a peg belay in a small corner 3 metres right of the ledge and trees of the first stance of Sarabanda Allucinogena.

2.   25m 5b. Climb the slab to a shallow crack, up this to a niche. Follow the diagonal crack/ramp right to a large flake, then return leftwards to a stance with chains - i.e. the second abseil point.

3.   30m 5a. Diagonally left to a bolt, then diagonally rightwards via second bolt to a stance at the abseil trees. (This pitch can be

climbed direct - harder and unprotected.)

Sarabanda Allucinogena   70m E1 5b
   Grassi & Lang 12/82

Perhaps the best slab climb at Caprie, taking a direct line to the right of Flutti Ipnotici.

1.   25m 5a. Diagonally rightwards to a pegbolt, move up to another bolt and follow a flake to a peg (or direct from here at 5b, unprotected). Go diagonally right to a larger flake and follow this rightwards to another pegbolt. Grassy steps lead to trees and a stance with 2 bolts.

2.   25m 5a. Go diagonally right past 2 bolts. At the third go left to a flake and peg. Follow this (bolt) to its end. Continue more or less direct past 2 more bolts to another below the overlap. Belay here (Friends), or better, traverse left to the chains at the foot of the first abseil.

3.   20m 5b. From the bolt below it, climb directly over the overlap and continue more or less direct to the top, following the line of bolts to belay on the abseil tree.

FORESTO

Lying on the north side of the Susa Valley, the hillside behind the tiny village of Foresto is covered by a mass of limestone crags. To date only the three most accessible have been developed, and despite their close proximity the climbing on each cliff is of an entirely different nature; the narrow gorge of the Orrido has steep walls and overhangs, generally with large flat holds, the Paretine Bianche low angled friction climbs, and Striature Nere fierce technical problems very much in the modern idiom. The narrow walls of the Orrido keep it shaded for much of the day - an advantage in the height of summer when the sun is only on the face in the afternoons, although in spring and autumn it can make the rock rather cold. In contrast, the sunny south-facing Paretine and Striature Nera are ideal in spring and autumn, and are even climbable in winter, but are generally too hot for enjoyable summer climbing.

Note. High above Bussoleno is the hamlet of Chianocco. Beyond is the Orrido Chianocco (Nature Reserve), an even narrower gorge than that of Foresto, and another shady summer retreat, with a number of short, bolt-protected test-pieces on its bulging, pocketed walls. To protect rare bird species there is a voluntary ban on springtime climbing. Both Orridos have via ferratas leading beyond the climbing areas.

Access
Approaching from Turin on the N24/25, bear right for Bussoleno, and after another mile turn right for Foresto.

L'ORRIDO DI FORESTO

The climbing history of the Orrido began with the artificial ascent of Fessura Obliqua in the 1950's, although the major lines were not ascended until the 70's. These were still mainly artificial, but the visit of Frenchmen Berhault and Edlinger in June 1980 with an almost free ascent of Nani Verde (now 6b free), was a turning point for Italian climbing. Others, particularly Marco Bernardi, followed their example, and today all the climbs are completely free. The history of the actual gorge is far older; in medieval times it was used as a leper colony and the buildings remain in a remarkably well-preserved state. These *lazzaretto* are useful for locating routes, and the most leftward actually start from their roofs.

Although all the routes have in-situ protection, this tends to be well spaced, and with the flat holds and generally overhanging rock, the climbing can be a little intimidating on first acquaintance. The limestone has been partly metamorphosed to resemble marble, and although very solid in the lower half, it tends to deteriorate above. As a result the routes normally finish at abseil chains after 2 or 3 pitches. Because of the overhanging nature of the wall, climbing is often possible even during rain.

Approach
Coming into Foresto turn left across a bridge over the stream, then immediately right. Park in a small square at the end of the road. A narrow footpath leads along the river bank into the gorge - 2 minutes to the foot of the routes.

Nani Verdi   60m E5 6b
   Galante, Grassi & Sacco 3/74
Start immediately right of the right-hand building, below an obvious finger crack leading diagonally rightwards.

Orrido di Foresto.

1 - Nani Verdi 60m E5 6b
2 - Fessura Obliqua 85m VS 4b
3 - Arcobalena Controculturale 50m E3 6a
4 - Suspiria

1.   20m 6b. Climb the crack (many pegs) and take the roof above on its right. Continue up a small corner, then go right to a second roof. Over this with difficulty and move left and up to a stance.
2.   40m 6a. Up to the roof above the stance and over this slightly leftwards. Easier climbing leads diagonally rightwards to a ledge. Traverse a little left to the last large roof visible from below. Heave over this and climb the wall above to a stance. Abseil off.

Some metres right is a large diagonal chimney crack - the Fessura Obliqua. Immediately left of this is **Pulcinastro** (2 pitches of 6b and 6a, but said to be 7a at the start if you're less than 5ft. 7ins!). The first pitch moves right at about 4 or 5 metres, but a direct variant - **Strenuous**, 6c+ Bernardi '84 - gives the hardest pitch at Foresto - another of the 1986 'top 30' Italian climbs.

Fessura Obliqua   85/130m VS 4b
   Beily, Cech & Viero 1950's
A polished classic. As the wide section of crack is avoided on the right, the climbing is less thrutchy and much better than it looks.
1.   35m 4b. Follow the line of the crack - mainly by its right edge - to a stance below a flared corner.
2.   35m 4b. Follow the crack to a white wall. Climb this to belay in a niche.
3.   15m 4a. Either follow the crack all the way to a stance on a ledge, or better, make 2 diversions rightwards to climb the right arête to the same point.

Either abseil from here, or continue to the top by 3 pitches of 20, 15 and 10m at a similar standard. On the first of these it is better to avoid the overhanging section of the crack (5a) by an exposed traverse right below small roofs, before climbing a white wall to belay left of a large roof.

Starting with a thin finger crack, and sharing its stances, the rounded arête immediately right of the first 2 pitches of Fessura Obliqua, is taken by **Elefante Rosa**   70m E4 6a, 5c. (M.Bernardi '82).

Five metres right of the chimney of Fessura Obliqua, and with a particularly fine second pitch up the scooped slab right of the second pitch of Elefante is:

Arcobalena Controculturale   50m E3 6a
   Grassi & Zimaglia 8/79
1.   30m 4c. Climb the wall more or less directly at first, move slightly left, then back diagonally right to belay on a good ledge.
2.   20m 6a. The pocketed slab/wall left of pitch 2 of Suspiria, to

belay as for that route.

About ten metres right of Fessura Obliqua is another large, right-ward slanting crack, the **Fessura Facile** (VS 4c - care required with loose rock at the end of pitch 1). Starting up the rib just left of this, and giving superbly varied climbing is:

Suspiria 72m E4 6a

1984

1. 30m 5a. Easily up the rib, then traverse almost horizontally right. Follow the steep wall to a roof and pull over this leftwards to a stance.

2. 17m 6a. Traverse right along the ledge, and climb up to the sling on the roof above on big holds (which now run out). Gain a standing position on the large flat block and make hard moves up the steep slabby wall to a bolt. Go horizontally left to chains.

3. 25m 5c. Climb the wall leftwards to a small roof split by a crack. Cross this rightwards and move over a second small roof to an obvious 'V' niche in a larger one. Over this (2 bolts - easier than it looks) and up to chains.

Note: **Strapiombini** (5c) takes the overhangs directly above the first stance, finishing at the second stance of Arcobaleno.

Descent

2 abseils. 1) 25m to second stance. 2) 40m free to ground.

Further upstream the path finishes at a concrete weir. Beyond this a steep wall rises directly from the water. All four one pitch routes squeezed into this section of rock start from boulders in the river, and both keeping the ropes dry and regaining the boulders from abseil would be a good officer selection test. Belay bolt in boulder on far bank.

All the routes are worthwhile. Following lines of bolts these are, from left to right:

Shock E2 5c.

Gnomo Buono E2 5c.

Macho Man E4 6a.

Starts a metre right of the above and climbs directly to its stance.

29 Ottobre E3 6a.

Takes the obvious water-worn scoop to the right.

LE PARETINE BIANCHE DI MARMO

To the right of Foresto is a continuous line of cliffs; low down and visible from much of the village, are the white slabs of the Paretine. Coming into the village of Foresto turn right, and after about 200m take the track on the left. Follow this for about 100m to where it steepens and bears around to the left, and park. The track itself leads up to a disused marble quarry, and beyond this a good viewpoint overlooking the Orrido; whereas the Paretine is visible to the right. Take the path leading off to the right and follow it for about 400m to the top of the crag, where an easy path leads down to its foot.

Roughly 50m wide and 40m in height, the once-quarried face bears over 20 routes and variants. With the exception of the low friction of the marble, the climbing is somewhat reminiscent of Baggy Point. The older climbs are protected by pegs and pegbolts, the newer ones mainly by spits.

STRIATURE NERE

Follow the path as above, but continue past the top of the Paretine for another 200m. The foot of the wall is hidden by trees, but once beyond these the cliff is easily recognizable by the near vertical black stripes that give it its name.

With the exception of a few 2 pitch routes, the climbs are of 1 pitch to in-situ abseil points. About 100m wide and 100m high, the cliff is formed of 2 parts - a left and a right-hand section. Between the two there is usually a wooden notice board with a list of routes and their grades. As many have the names painted at their foot, it is an easy matter to identify the climbs.

As with so many areas, the full potential of this wall was only realized with the advent of 'spit-rock', and with over 20 of the 30 plus routes graded 6a and above, Striature Nere is now one of the most important outcrops in Italy. Marco Bernardi and Andrea Gallo have been prominent in recent developments, and three of their routes appeared in 1986's 'top 30' (Funeral Party, Luna and Bel Vivere - all 6c/7a).

The routes are, from left to right:

Mimose Appasite   5a. (needs nuts)

Mafalda   5a/b.

Striature Nere

Avril 5b.

Bel Vivere 6c/6c.

Ventre di Parigi 5c/6a.

Hallowe'en 1. 6a. 2. 6a.

Creme Caramel 1. 6a+. 2. 5b+.

Luna 6c/7a.

Technologica 1. 6c. 2. 6a.

Senza Parole 6a.

1 Fix Tcen Tcen 6a.

Blues Brothers 6b.

Mal di Pancia 6b.

Muppet Show 6a+.

Reginetta delle Neri 5c.

Phenomena 5c.

Fessura dell Tentativo 5b/c.

Fahrenheit 451 6a.

Fermenti Lattici 6c. (Direct start at same grade)

Sex Crime 6b.

Egomania 5c.

Dedalus 6a.

Rio 6b.

Arrakis 1. 5c/6a. 2. 5b+.

Falce dello Scorpione Turchino 1. 5a. 2. 5b/c.

Verra La Morte 6c.

Gorilla Lilla 6a+

Funeral Party 6c.

Pronfipiede 6b+.

Tirsys 5c/6a.

Spiral Yetty 6a. (Direct finish 5c+)

Piglia Mosche 5c+

BARDONECCHIA
PARETE DEI MILITI

The Italian ski resort of Bardonecchia lies very close to the Italian/ French border, although the great limestone wall of Militi is on the French side in the Valle Stretta. However, as the only real access is by road from Bardonecchia, the area is best considered as a part of Italy. Certainly it is viewed as such by the climbers of Turin and the Valley Susa who have been responsible for its development.

With a summit height of almost 2,000 metres the 350 metre high north face of Militi is Dolomitic in both scale and character, and the first climbs of the 40's and 50's by such famous names as Gervassuti and Rivero, were very much of an alpine nature, following obvious natural lines and with their fair share of loose rock. The free-climbing wave of the '80's brought a re-appraisal of the area, and a realization of the potential of the band of solid limestone at the foot of the extreme right of the face. Most of the routes described here date from 1984/85, and although development is continuing, there seems to be little likelihood of a guidebook in the near future. All the routes are well equipped with bolts and belay/abseil chains, with names (and sometimes simple topos) usually painted below. Two or three hundred metres left of the main area is the competition crag (La Mura di Gare). The routes here were artificially created for the competition extravaganzas of '85 and '86, and offer a number of 1 pitch test-pieces, mostly of 6b and above. As they are generally unnamed and have little aesthetic appeal the routes are not described here, although the approach is given for those who wish to explore them for themselves.

With its restricted number of climbs Militi is not a major climbing centre. However, all the climbs described are worthwhile, with the best potential classics - and as they can all be reached in a matter of minutes from either tent or car, a good E point score can easily be attained. Add the excellent free camping in a beautiful high valley with something of the feel of Tuolumne Meadows, and it becomes either a convenient stopping-off point between France and Italy, or a pleasant part of a tour of the crags of Susa or Piemonte. N.E. facing, climbing is only possible from May to October.

Access and Approach

Bardonecchia is easily accessible from France via the tunnel from
Frejus, or less easily from Briancon via the col de Montgenevre and
Claviere. The latter approach joining the N24 from Susa/Turin at
Sauze d'Oulx. As one enters Bardonecchia from Sauze, turn left,
and then left again to follow signs for Melezet, reaching the French
border 3 miles from the town. This is manned only on the Italian
side, and you may be required to produce the usual travel docu-
ments (passport, green card etc.). Two miles of reasonable gravel-
led track lead to numerous parking places near the foot of the cliff,
with a wide choice of camping in the meadows and pine trees.

For the competition crag take the track forking off left just
before the picnic site. The crag has a large cave below and left, and
excavated platforms for stances in the scree cone at its foot. The
track continues for a further mile (passing a farm selling butter and
cheese) to a tiny hamlet with two rifugios, a bar and restaurant.

The main climbing area starts at the obvious arête at the right of
the cliff, and continues for about 100 metres leftwards. 20 metres
left of the arête is a small pillar with rockfall debris at its foot. This
gives the line of: **Minuetto**   20m HVS 5b. Hardest at the start.

Just left of the pillar is:
Crono   40m E2 5c
(The first pitch makes a worthwhile HVS)
1.   25m 5a. The steep wall has a bulge at half-height. Go left to
belay as for Incontro, or continue to make a 40m pitch.
2.   15m 5c. Climb the smooth rib on the right, and continue to
chains.

10m left again is a steep wall below a ledge and small tree.
Above this is a superb sheet of Verdon-like white limestone, taken
by the second pitches of the next 2 climbs.

Incontro   55m E1 5b
1.   25m 5b. Pass an awkward bulge at 10m and belay on the left
below a tree.
2.   30m 5b. Climb up to the left of the tree, up a rib and move left
into a groove/crack. Follow this (sustained), to belay chains at its
top.

(**Specchio**, a variant pitch 2, moves diagonally left before returning rightwards to the same final stance - 6c.)

Further left is an obvious pillar with a pine tree above.

Albatros   60m E3 6a
   Pirona & Bernardi '84

The left-hand end of Militi. Climbers on Tao. Abseil rope shows line of Locale per il Cielo.

63

1.   25m 4c. Fairly direct up the pillar to chains. (As for pitch 1 of the old classic Rondine which takes the couloir line to the left.)

2.   35m 6a. Pass the flake above and right, by a small roof on its right. Continue by the discontinuous crack line, with hard moves to reach the prominent jam-crack where it re-appears.

(It is usual to abseil from here, although several pitches continue above. The first of these is said to be 6c and poorly protected, although several bolts can be seen from the stance.)

Further left is a low pillar taken by a 20m Severe. Left of this is a clean wall, approx. 25m wide and 25m high, capped by roofs. Just left of the corner formed by the junction of wall and pillar is:

Musudocet   25m HVS 5b

Following the bolts more or less direct - good sustained, climbing.

2m left is:

Tao   90m E4/5 6b - or 35m E3 6a
   R.Pirona '84

A tremendously varied route on excellent rock.

1.   25m 5c. Straight up to chains.

2.   10m 6a. Diagonally leftwards via several small roofs, before a difficult horizontal traverse leads to a ledge.

Either abseil from here or:

3.   20m 6b. Beautiful slab climbing diagonally leftwards.

4.   35m 5c. The wall above.

3m left again and taking the lower roof almost direct, is:

Locale per il Cielo   E1/2 5b/c
   FA 26/7/86

I top-roped this the day after it had been cleaned, and the provisional gradings reflect the fact that it was still rather dusty and had not been completely bolted. The lower roof feels massively suspect, but the climbing is good.

Left again are 2 routes with a common first pitch.

Nonna Abelarda   56m E5 6c
   M.Bernardi '84

1.   28m 5c. Direct to chains under roof.

2.   28m 6c. Diagonally left under roof to chains.

Rebecca   43m E6 6c
   M.Bernardi '84

One of the 1985 'top 30' listed routes in Italy, by August '86 it had received only 1 repeat.

1.   As for Nonna Abelarda.

2. 15m 6c.Direct over roofs above - protected only by small Friends.

Just left is another low pillar, with the furthest route to the left starting from its top.

Sendero Luminoso   40m E5 6c

1.   20m. Easily to the top of the pillar.

2.20m 6c. Direct up the slabby wall via bolts to chain.

ROCCA SBARUA

Sbarua is the most popular of the classic climbing areas within easy reach of Turin, and has been described as a symbol of Piemontese climbing. At weekends it throngs with a healthy mixture of ages, styles and abilities - alpinists in helmets and breeches rubbing shoulders with lycra-clad rock-jocks in a friendly atmosphere somewhat akin to Stanage on a Sunday afternoon. However, unlike Stanage it has yet to be discovered by the MSC and mid-week climbing can be enjoyed in glorious seclusion. With its beautiful setting high above the beech and chestnut woods looking across the plain to the mountains beyond, and its excellent rough grey granitoid gneiss, it is easy to understand why this complex of slabs and pillars inspires such affection. There is a wealth of climbing in the lower grades, with the older classics - such as the Gervasutti route - following superb natural lines.

Those that once employed aid have been freed to give a number of three star routes in the lower extreme grades, and the use of 'spits' has led to more modern classics of a similar difficulty and quality on the previously untouched slabs and arêtes. As yet there is little to attract the climber operating above 6a, and though the freeing of the remaining aid pitches - particularly those on the 'great wall' of the Placche Gialle - may result in a small number of super routes, it is to be hoped that the blank slabs do not become criss-crossed with a meaningless collection of bolt ladders. Most routes are very well protected by pegs and/or bolts, although a few small/medium nuts or Friends may sometimes be useful.

Despite its base height of just over 1,000 metres, Sbarua's sunny southern aspect means that climbing is possible virtually throughout the year - even sometimes when snow covers the ground. However, the best months are spring and autumn when the colours of the trees are as attractive as the climbing, the summer months being generally considered too hot for comfort. Having said that, a breezy day following a period of stormy

ROCCA SBARUA

- Placche Gialle
2 Sperone Rivero
3 Torrione Grigio
4 Sperone Cinquetti
5 Torre del Bimbo

weather gave us an excellent day in late August '87.

Access, Camping etc.
Access is from Pinerolo, 35km south-west of Turin on the N23.
This road continues to Sestriere and Claviere, thus also giving
access from France via either Briancon or Bardonecchia. From
Pinerolo take the dead end road north to the small village of Talucco (about 4 miles, trattoria recommended). Continue for another
mile to an obvious fork in the road. From here there are two possibilities (1) at weekends, Bank Holidays etc. take the right-hand
fork and follow this to its end and park. A path continues more or
less in the line of the road past some houses. Follow this steeply to
the Colle Ciardonet, then take the right-hand of the two paths
leading down into the trees and follow a well-marked track to the
Rifugio Melano (signposted at the colle, about 30 minutes from the
parking place). (2) Mid-week it is possible to take the left fork and
follow the road steeply around a number of sharp bends until a
bumpy track leads off to the right signposted 'Casa Dairin' and
'Colle del Cro'. Follow this with care until it ends in a tiny hamlet,
turn here and return some way to park at the side of the track - *DO
NOT PARK IN THE HAMLET*. A fairly level walk of about 5 minutes
leads through the houses to the Colle Ciardonet, and thus to the
Rifugio (20 minutes in total). This is particularly useful for those
intending to camp at the Colle as there is a fresh water fountain in
the hamlet.

The Colle Ciardonet is often used for camping and has several
good, flat, open spaces. It is also likely that permission would be
granted for camping in the meadows bordering the road from
Pinerolo, this should be sought either in Talucco or the houses near
to the first described parking area. It would also be reasonably
easy to reach Sbarua from the campsites in Bussoleno or Avigliana
(about 1 hour's drive - see La Valle Susa). The Rifugio Milano has
35 beds and is open at weekends and public holidays from
October to June, including winter when conditions are favourable.
The rifugio also serves meals and contains the new routes book.

N.B. In very dry summers there may be no water available either
from the hut or the hamlet. In such circumstances a more reliable
fountain can be found on the path leading up from the Colle Ciardonet to the Colle Sperina, i.e. the left-hand path. This is also a
pleasant walk for non-climbing members of a party.

At the time of writing a new (and badly needed) guidebook is in
preparation which should appear early in 1988. The existing

guidebook is still useful for the older classics and can be obtained from the: Club Alpino Italiano, Via Barbaroux 1, Turin.

Rocca Sbarua e Monte Tre Denti by Gian Piero Motti, 1969.

Approach and Descent

From the rifugio the huge yellowish wall of the Placche Gialle is clearly visible, bounded on its left by the Spigolo Centrale (central arête). Most of the routes described here lie either very close to this arête, or in the area to the left of this - Sbarua Centrale. From the left side of the rifugio a path leads up to the foot of the large boulder which forms the foot of the Spigolo Centrale. This is topped by an iron memorial cross. The path continues leftwards to ascend a gully which forms the main descent path (some scrambling, equipped with chains in some places). At the top of this is a massive pile of stacked flakes topped by an easy angled slab with an obvious white quartz vein running up it. This vein is the line of **Vena di Quarzo** (20m 4a), an enjoyable Severe protected by pegbolts - near the top move first left, then right to finish, or exit direct at 5a/b (1 bolt). Abseil off from chain above. This can be combined with **Ellena** (15m 5a), the unprotected left arête of the leaning boulder below the stacked flakes. Another worthwhile pitch is the roof-capped corner to the left: **Interval Training** (35m 5c). The corner-groove leads to the roof, which is much easier than it looks. Follow the slab above to finish at the chains of Vena di Quarzo - carry several medium nuts.

The pillar to the right of the Spigolo Centrale is the Sperone Rivero, two climbs are described on this and one on the Torrione Grigio which lies behind it. Right again are the Sperone Cinquetti and the Torre del Bimbo which contain a number of popular routes in the lower grades, as well as several new spit-protected climbs. Unfortunately we have not, as yet, had the opportunity to explore these.

Sbarua Centrale

Via Gervasutti   110m Hard Severe 4b

  Gervasutti & Ronco 1935

Perhaps the best of the easier classics. Medium sized nuts may be useful, particularly in the final corner.

Below and right of the boulder topped by the cross is a reddish corner trending rightwards.

1.   35m 4a. Follow the corner exiting right to a huge flake. Climb

ROCCA SBARUA

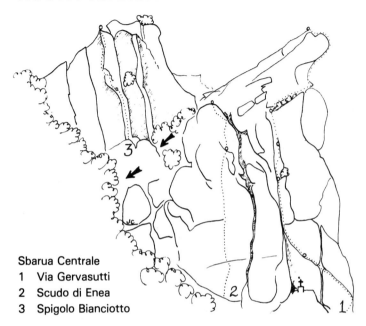

Sbarua Centrale
1 Via Gervasutti
2 Scudo di Enea
3 Spigolo Bianciotto

this and make an exposed traverse rightwards on more flakes to a ledge with a tree. Move up slightly, scramble left along a ledge and move up to a large ledge with a huge ring peg. (Also the stance for 'Voyage'.)

2. 40m 4a. Move easily diagonally leftwards to the obvious corner on the left of the slabs. Belay here or continue up the corner to its top.

3. 20m 4a. Trend rightwards to the foot of the final corner.

4. 20m 4b. The celebrated 'Diedro Gervasutti'. Climb this enjoyably by bridging, jamming or laybacking.

Walk left to reach the descent path, or walk right for 20 metres until below a large roof at the edge of the arête. Climb the chimney to the right of this (20m 4a) to reach the summit blocks - continue by Ellena/Vena di Quarzo.

Voyage Selon les Classiques   80m E3 6a

Marco de Marchi 1980's

Three enjoyably sustained pitches of Tremadoc-like slab climbing lead to a difficult finish. Superb. Completely equipped, although a few medium nuts are useful for the cracks of pitches 2 and 4.

Start by scrambling right from the iron cross to a beech tree in a large crack. Voyage starts up the slab to the right of this.

1.   15m 5b. Climb the slab - first on the right near the arête, then moving left before finishing direct. Large ring bolt on ledge.

2.   25m 5b. The obvious slab right of the corner of Gervasutti. Follow bolts to gain a small corner crack at half-height. Up this to exit right at a ledge. Belay here or continue by:

3.   15m 5b/c. The slab right of the layback crack of Gervasutti. Start up a flake on the right and follow bolts to a ledge.

4.   25m 6a. Climb the slab to below a crack - make a difficult move to gain this and follow it to an awkward exit.

Either walk off left to gain the descent path, or scramble up and right to the top of a huge block. Between the chimney on the right and the huge roof on the left is an overhanging crack. This is:

Belvedere   25m 5c.

An initial section of off-width leads to excellent jamming. Move right and over blocks to exit - spit protection. Walk down the ridge to the left to gain the descent path.

Spigolo Centrale   80m 5b

Start from the ledge above the first pitch of Gervasutti and Voyage. Move around the arête to the right onto the main face, and belay on a peg below a short wall. Small nuts are now required for this wall as it has recently been de-pegged - with the exception of one peg at the crux.

Strenuous and exposed climbing leads up a line of cracks, grooves and corners, sometimes to the left of the arête and sometimes to the right. Finish on the final ledge of Voyage and descend or continue as for that route.

The route can be started lower down by a pitch following the obvious line of bolts to the right of the first corner of Gervasutti. Only recently equipped (autumn 1987) and mostly overhanging, this gives good jamming until parallel cracks lead rightwards to the tree at the end of the traverse of pitch 1 of Gervasutti. Follow this route to the first stance. **Bauhaus** (20m 6a/b - De Marchi 1980's) is an alternative third pitch.

Just left of the iron cross is an area of slabs. The steep wall forming the right edge of these (more or less immediately above the cross) gives the short **Paparetta Show** (5c), and the easy angled cracks on the right of the slabs via **Via Normale** (Diff). Left again is **Torinesi** (Severe), and taking the centre of the good slab the enjoyable:

Scudo di Enea   50m HVS 5a or 60m E1 5b
   M.De Marchi & A.Parodi 1980's
Protected by fairly spaced bolts and pegs - carry a few small nuts and Friends.
1.   50m 5a. Climb the centre of the slab to a small roof (possible stance). Cross this just to the left of its right edge and continue up the slab left of the cracks of Torinesi to belay at a ledge with a large ring-peg.
   Abseil off or continue by:
2.   10m 5b. The line of bolts above with a short harder section near the arête.
   Abseil off chains - or walk left to gain the descent path at a chained section. Above and left is a series of arêtes and grooves, and a fine tower with a cracked slabby right wall. The wall and arête give:

Spigolo Bianciotto   30m E1 5b
   L.Bianciotto 1949
Walk up the descent path a little way to a group of beech trees - traverse left to the foot of the cracked wall.
1.   20m 5b. Climb a small arête between two shallow corners to reach a dirt ledge. Move left and climb cracks on the wall until it is possible to move left onto the arête. Move up then back right to belay on a ledge below a roof.
2.   10m 5a. Move up left to the roof, then go over this on the left to gain the arête. Climb this, first on the left, then on the right.
   Abseil from chains or walk right and follow the path upwards to continue by Ellena/Vena di Quarzo. The line of spits up the wall right of Bianciotto is **Flash Gordon** (5c).
   The Spigolo Bianciotto can also be approached from the iron cross at the foot of the Spigolo Centrale by walking up the descent path. Some way to the left of the cross are two large boulders. The upper is reached by following the descent path past the start of Scudo di Enea until a small path forks off to the left. Scramble along this then down to the foot of the upper boulder. This is split by two obvious cracks, the left an off-width - **Fessura del Nero** 6a, the right an excellent jamcrack - **Vietato Soffiare** 5c. On the lower

boulder is **Incubus a Manhattan** (5c).

Sperone Rivero

Approach

From the right-hand end of the hut a path leads across the hill to a large Pant-Ifan-type boulder scree. Go up this trending right then follow a small path rightwards to the foot of the cliff. (The left arête of this gives the excellent Severe, **Via Rivero** 150m - spaced pegs, carry nuts and Friends.) Follow the path rightwards to where 'Bon Ton' is painted on the rock. The combination of a climb on the Sperone Rivero and the Motti-Grassi on the Torrione Grigio gives a superb day's climbing.

Bon Ton   135m E1 5c (110m HVS 5a)

Enjoyable climbing, despite an excess of bolts and a rather artificial line. Pitch 5 is much harder than the rest of the climb, and the first 4 pitches make a good HVS.

1.   35m 5a. Climb over the bulge (pegs) and make a rising leftward traverse to belay at a small oak tree.

2.   25m 5a. Climb the wall immediately right of the tree, then follow grooves to a slab below a ledge with belay chains.

3.   25m 5a. Climb the slab right of a dirty gully by a crack. Move over the overlap to a belay.

4.   25m 5a. Move back left and over detached flakes to the foot of a large crack leading to a tree - stance with chains above the tree. At HVS abseil from here, or move horizontally leftwards to finish easily by the Via Rivero - only worthwhile if wishing to do the Motti-Grassi route.

   (N.B. With 50m ropes it is just possible to combine pitches 3 & 4, although this necessitates belaying at the foot of the tree - note the peg!)

5.   25m 5c. The obvious arête above the tree. Sustained, fingery climbing, but with excellent spit protection.

   Go 10/15m left to a large peg and scramble to the top of the pillar.

Nani Acidi   100m E2 5c

A more sustained route with excellent climbing following a natural line. Start some way to the right of Bon Ton at an arrow scratched on the rock.

1.   35m 5a. Easily up to reach a slab. Continue with more difficulty to a stance on a large ledge.

2.   45m 5b/c. The short wall on the right leads to a flake. Layback this to reach a line of bolts leading diagonally rightwards across the slab to below a roof. Make a hard pull to overcome this and continue up a line of weakness to a stance below an overlap.

3.   20m 5c. Move delicately right around the overlap, then more easily upwards to belay at chains.

From here either abseil the route, or - for the Motti-Grassi - continue by another 45m pitch of V.Diff. standard to the top of the pillar.

Behind, and clearly visible, is the grey pillar of the Torrione Grigio. Descend the gully leading from the top of the Sperone Rivero, keeping left to reach a large ledge. Follow this rightwards, passing a huge flake-corner. Between this and the right arête is a crack system behind the central of 3 chestnut trees. This is the start of the:

Via Motti-Grassi   115m E2 5b/AO(E3 6a free)
   Motti & Grassi January 1966

A fine, strenuous route. In late October '87 the in-situ pegs were very old and a selection of small to medium nuts and Friends was necessary. However, according to a reliable source, the route was re-equipped with spits just a few weeks after our ascent. If so the climb may now be rather easy for its grade, although on a weekday with no other climbers on the cliff, it has an air of remoteness.

1.   20m 5b. Climb the crack to an ancient peg. Traverse left and climb strenuously up steep rock to belay on 3 old pegs (and nuts) at the start of a leftward diagonal crack.

2.   15m 5a. Follow the diagonal crack leftwards to its end. Belay on two old pegs at a ledge slightly to the left.

3.   15m 5b/AO (6a free). Return right and climb a steep crack. Traverse right to the foot of an undercut rib - above is a peg-bolt with (hopefully) a long sling. Use the sling to reach a peg in the roof above - or free-climb the groove on the right (6a - serious if relying only on the peg-bolt, but this is said to have been replaced by a spit). Move right over the roof with the help of a monster jug, and belay immediately above by a tree.

4.   30m 5a. Up and slightly left following pegs, then make a long diagonal traverse left following more pegs. An excellent pitch.

5.   35m 4c. Diagonally left at first, returning right to cross a bulge to enter a corner. Climb this to its top. Move right and climb up to, then over, a large horizontal flake. Move easily up and diagonally leftwards, then traverse horizontally left to a stance on a ledge - block and nut belays. It is very difficult to avoid rope drag on this

pitch. Scramble up to trees to finish.

Descent

Walk left to pass below a small rock buttress. Scramble up through woods on the left of this, ascending diagonally rightwards to aim for the high point of the ridge. Go along this to the left and descend its left side to reach a rock nose at the top of the Vena di Quarzo slab - hidden abseil chain on the left of the rock. Make a 20m abseil to the top of the huge stacked flakes above the finish of Gervasutti/Voyage. Climb down to the left of these (facing out) then follow the normal descent path.

The start of the Motti-Grassi can also be reached by the gully between the Sperone Rivero and the next tower - the Sperone Cinquetti (30 minutes from the rifugio). Starting around the arête to the right of this route is the **Via Barbi** (110m 5b). Starting with two pitches of 5b and then easing to VS standard, this takes a wandering line to the left and right of the arête and is said to be very worthwhile.

FINALE

In recent years, it seems likely that more British climbers have visited Finale than all the other areas in this guidebook put together - initially perhaps because of the proximity of France. It was the magic of Verdon that first opened the eyes of hundreds to the pleasures of solid, pocketed limestone. The ripples spread outwards through Provence to St. Jeannet, then along the coast to Monaco and Finale. The language may be different, but the rock is as good as anything in Provence - and Finale has something more. The three river valleys which unite in the Riviera resort of Finale Ligure, have carved a limestone plateau into a profusion of cliffs - almost as if all the limestone of the Peak District were compressed into an area some 5 kilometres square - a climber's paradise. Yet although climbing began in the late 60's, it was the opening of the Ventimiglia autostrada that really stimulated development, the elevated sections of motorway giving superb views of the crags and their potential.

A dozen cliffs and almost 200 routes were described in the '83 guidebook, but since then others have been developed, and the number of routes has probably doubled. Some half-dozen cliffs are approaching maturity, but even Monte Cucco, the most popular of these, continues to produce a regular quota of new routes, and it will be a long time before the supply of rock begins to run out. As Pete Gomersall noted in 1984, the area has a great wealth of climbing for the middle grade climber, although at that time there was only a limited menu for those operating at 'solid 6b'. This has certainly changed and although many new routes are still in the 5b to 6b range, an increasing number are from 6c upwards, so that today there is a wide choice for all climbers of VS and above.

All the cliffs described here can be reached in twenty minutes or less - Monte Cucco in only two or three. But all have very different characteristics and atmospheres, from the long two hundred metre plus routes of Bric Pianarella with its views out over the sea, to the superb technical walls of Rocca di Corno. Their low altitude and

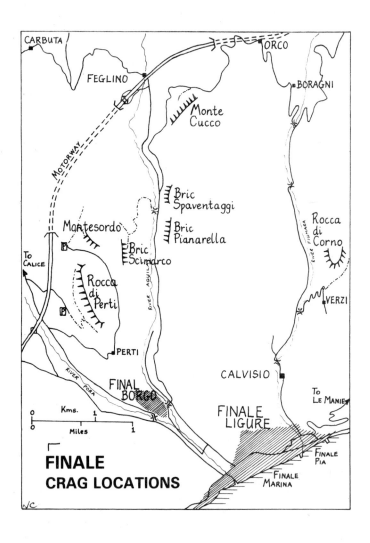

FINALE
CRAG LOCATIONS

different aspects allow climbing throughout the year - and it is often possible to find sun or shade by a judicious choice of venue. Even a hot August day can offer shady climbing on Cucco in the morning, followed by a relaxing swim in the silky waters of the Mediterranean, making this an ideal area for the family climber. For non-climbers there is also a network of scenic footpaths, often following ancient tracks linking once-inhabited caves and Roman antiquities. However, spring and autumn are the optimum times, for although Christmas can be good, the chances of rain and cold winds make winter visits something of a gamble - and though rare, snow is not completely unknown.

Above all Finale is a place for the pure enjoyment of climbing - few of the routes are really serious, and as many of the older peg-protected routes are being re-equipped with 10mm 'super-spits' (e.g Aspettando al Sole, Adele and Fessura Machetto) this seems likely to continue. Peak-time overcrowding is an inevitable consequence of the area's growing continental popularity, and at such times the exploration of lesser crags such as Bric Scimarco or Monte Sordo is well worthwhile.

Note: Access for Scimarco has changed since the '83 guide-book. Surrounded by trees, the cliff is high up on the side of the valley facing Bric Pianarella and gets sun in the mornings. Park near the tiny roadside chapel as for Pianarella, cross the bridge and follow a track past a house. A winding path (marked by red painted diamonds) is followed for 20 minutes to a fork. Take the left fork leading downwards (path now marked by a triangle of red spots) to the foot of the cliff - an interesting 30 minutes. The classic line of **Il Traverso** (E1/2 5c) gives excellent climbing, with a newer direct finish (**Cuneo** 6a?) up a pillar. The VSs of **Il Cinghiale** and **Pilastro del Re** look worthwhile and there are several new routes up the slab to the left of the latter, including an excellent E1.

Approach, Camping etc.
The autostrada Ventimiglia gives easy access from France and Monaco to the west, Genoa to the east and motorways from Milan and Turin. About 3 hours from climbing areas of southern France. The best direct route from Britain is Belgium - Luxembourg - Basel - St. Gotthard Tunnel - Milan. When approaching from the east (Savona etc.) take the Feglino exit. From France, exit for Finale. It is not possible to exit to Feglino when going east, or to obtain west-bound access to the motorway from Feglino.

There is free camping below Monte Cucco, with water available from a roadside fountain. At present it is possible to camp rough in several other locations, and to bivouac close to some crags. However, there are said to be plans to give the area some kind of special status (National Park etc.) so this may change. In any case it is always necessary to take the strictest precautions to avoid any chance of starting fires. These can quickly become uncontrollable in the dry Mediterranean scrub, and have devasted areas of southern France in recent years. A number of campsites with full facilities are to be found around Finale Ligure - 'Camping San Martino' at Le Manie (signposted from Finale Pia) is said to be good, and reasonably priced by Riviera standards.

Shops are plentiful in Finale Ligure (including one for Camping Gaz near the railway station), but parking is often a problem and the interesting medieval streets of Final Borgo, and a more restful alternative. There is a climbing shop in Borgo, and another in Feglino with an impressive array of tights and glitter chalk bags. Both stock the guidebook:

Finale - Andrea Gallo, pub. Melograno April 1987.

Like its predecessor *La Pietra di Finale* (Parodi and Grillo 1983), this is a topo-style guide with French tech-gradings.

There is also a cheaply printed German guidebook available from the climber's bar just outside the old town walls of Finale Borgo. Containing a selection of about 300 of the 600 odd routes now in existence, it similarly utilizes topos and the French grading system.

Kletterfuhrer Finale - Martin Lochner.

Mention should be made of the numerous village *ristorante,* where the food is often cheap and of high quality. Explore these for yourself!

MONTE CUCCO

Undoubtedly the major cliff of the area, with a huge number of high quality routes from 4b to 7b, easy access and camping below the crag, it is not surprising that Monte Cucco is also the most popular. At bank-holidays and peak weekends the cliff seethes with an international mix of cragrats worthy of a climbing EEC, with an atmosphere similar to Stoney or Tremadoc, although its size ensures that it can normally absorb large numbers of climbers. Facing NE, it offers welcome shade in the hotter months - in August the sun is only fully on the face from mid-afternoon.

Over 100 metres in height, and some 800 metres wide, Cucco

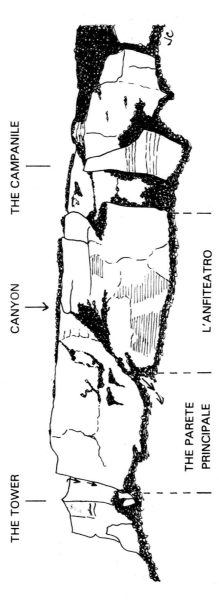

THE CAMPANILE

CANYON

THE TOWER

L'ANFITEATRO

THE PARETE PRINCIPALE

MONTE CUCCO

is clearly visible from the Feglino exit of the autostrada, its immense structure dividing conveniently into several obvious sectors. Starting from the left, about a third of the way along is the obvious feature of the La Torre - the tower - with a large open corner on its right (at the back of which is the steep descent gully). Right of this is the Parete Principale or main wall, defined on its right by the second descent route, the Canyon. Right of this is the aptly named L'Anfiteatro with the tower of the Campanile on its right.

Approach

Take the Orco turning from the Final Borgo - Feglino road. (Approaching from the autostrada this entails a sharp turning left about a mile after Feglino.) Just after a ruined building on the right, a rough track leads up to parking close to the foot of the cliff. However, at peak periods it is necessary to park on the road - there are plans to build a car park and toilets, both of which are badly needed. The track is now almost impassable for ordinary vehicles. vehicles.

Descent

For climbs near the tower, descend the steep corner gully (down-climbing of about V.Diff. standard, or abseil from chains). Otherwise follow a slightly descending path running rightwards parallel with the cliff edge (or left in the case of climbs in the Anfiteatro), for no more than 150m. Follow a path towards the edge and the top of the canyon should become obvious. Follow this rightwards until it becomes a gully, move left (facing out) and climb down easy rocks to the foot of the gully. As the plateau behind the cliff is a dense mass of scrub, if climbing here for the first time when daylight hours are short, it is as well to familiarize yourself with the descents whilst there is plenty of light!

La Torre

A number of 5c/6a routes climb the face below the obvious large ledge left of the tower, including **Enrico Quarto** - a worthwhile 5c with a hard start which follows a pocket line trending left towards the arête on the left (a direct on this is **Il Gattopardo** 7a). Starting a few metres right of the arête, the tower itself gives the excellent:

La Torre   70m HVS 5a
  Calcagno & Grillo 7/69

1. 30m 5a. Climb the wall and the crack above, move diagonally left to a thin corner and follow this more easily to a stance near the arête.
2. 35m 5a. Traverse several metres right and follow cracks more or less direct to the final overhang. Belay on a ledge. An alternative and slightly better finish is to move left and climb the exposed hanging flake almost level with the overhang. Other variations are possible lower down.
3. Scramble to the top.

Slightly right is another good line: **Mani d'Ora** E1 5b, 5a. The descent gully can be climbed at about V.Diff. and the face to the right has large holds/holes and two very worthwhile Severes.

Miguel 70m Severe 4a
   Casula et al 5/71
Starting a few metres right of the corner and taking a fairly direct line in 2 pitches, it saves its crux for the very top.

Luc 70m Severe 4a
   Calcagno et al 7/69
Climb the wall further right, to belay in a small cave. Exit before taking a diagonal rightward line to finish up a groove close to the right arête. (Carry nuts for P.2.)

The Parete Principale

The arête right of Luc is the start of the Parete Principale, and the next route takes a line just right of, with a stance on the arête. Originally climbed with the aid of sky-hooks is:
Banana Spit 70m E4 6b
   Ferrarsi & Parodi 2/82
Walk right and up on to a boulder to start.
1. 15m 6b. Move right across the slab, and climb a steep wall to a ledge. Belay here, or continue by;
2. 20m 6b. Follow the bulging wall to easy ground.

The overhanging wall below the start of Banana Spit is now taken by a direct start; **Banana Stranna** 7a, Gallo '85 (the first route at Finale to be given the French grade of 8a), and the obvious rightward slanting flakeline to the right is the strenuous start to:

Adele 80m E4 6a/b
   Calcagno & Croci '76
The wall above the flake is now well protected by bolts.

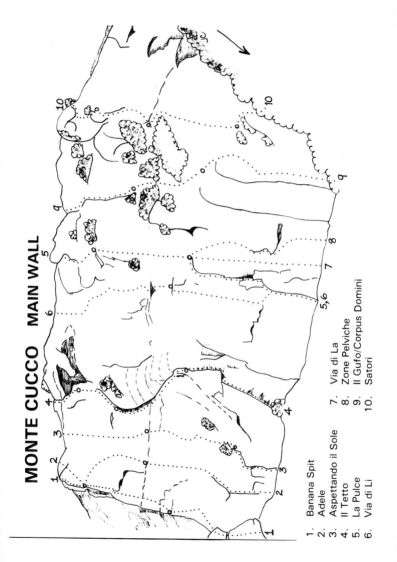

MONTE CUCCO MAIN WALL

1. Banana Spit
2. Adele
3. Aspettando il Sole
4. Il Tetto
5. La Pulce
6. Via di Li
7. Via di La
8. Zone Pelviche
9. Il Gufo/Corpus Domini
10. Satori

1.   40m 6a/b. Follow the flake past several pegs to its end. Climb the wall above trending right to gain a hairline crack, and follow this to a ledge.

2.   30m 5c. Follow the scoop/groove just right of the arête to an obvious traverse line (Grillomania), and follow this leftwards to belay on the arête.

3.   10m 4c. Trend right to finish.

Right again, starting from the left side of a ledge with trees is **Occhi Dolce per Frank Zappa** (25m French 7b). But starting from further right along the ledge, to follow a direct line in two long pitches is one of the most famous climbs at Finale. Beautiful climbing, only slightly marred by a rather polished crux.

Aspettando il Sole (Waiting for the Sun)   80m E4 5c, 6b

1.   15m 4b. Climb the short crack and arête to the ledge.

2.   25m 5c. Up the steep wall behind the tree, then the slab direct to a belay.

3.   40m 6b. Follow the line of bolts above, crossing the obvious traverse line (Grillomania E1 5b) to a hard finish. Plenty of quickdraws required! Can be split just below the traverse to give two 20 metres pitches of 5c and 6b.

Il Tetto   100m E1 5c (E1 5b A0)
Calcagno & Piotti 10/68

The obvious crack system below the large roof at the top of the crag provides a varied and enjoyable classic. Start at the foot of the obvious diagonal crack leading rightwards.

1.   30m 5a. Follow the crack, with a harder move to enter the vertical crack above. Up this on jugs to a stance.

2.   40m 5c.(just). Move leftwards with difficulty across the smooth black wall (crux), or use one or more pegs for aid, before laybacking up the crack on superb holds.

3.   20m 4c. The fine crack to a stance beneath the roof.

4.   10m 5b. Wild moves lead leftwards around the roof (pegs). A slightly easier finish takes the roof on the right.

La Pulce   100m VS 4c
Calcagno & Grillo 6/69

An almost direct line up the crack system to the right. Three pitches of: 1) 35m 4c.   2) 45m 4b.   3) 25m 4c.

Starting as for La Pulce to climb the difficult wall on the left, then a spectacular roof on superb holds, is the classic:
Via di Li   80m E1 5b/c

Grappiolo & Grillo 8/80

1. 30m 5b. As for La Pulce for 8m, moving left at a short diagonal crack. Climb the wall above for 20m, finally making hard moves right to belay.

2. 50m 5a. Up the steep wall above the belay to a roof. Cross this on large holds and gain a crack line. Follow this for 15m to ledges. Finish up the bulging wall on the left. (This pitch can be split at several places.)

To the right of La Pulce are **Via di La** 30m E2 5c, and **Zone Pelviche** 35m E1/2 5b - the latter moving up to an overlap, crossing this leftwards and continuing direct before moving left to belay as for di La. A direct on Pelviche is **Mi Dica Bravucci** 5c, and just right is **Training Sisters** E2 5c. The first corner to the right is the first pitch of **Corpus Domini** 5c, with an undercut start the slab to the right is **Toccata** and **Fugue** 5b, and the overhanging wall further right **Bucce d'Arancia** 6a.

As the corner is much harder than the rest of the climb, it is better to start Corpus Domini by the next corner right (as for Il Gufo):

Il Gufo/Corpus Domini 100m VS 4c

Calcagno & Grillo 69 & 71

1. 30m 4c. The corner to the right.

2. 25m. Move diagonally left then easily up to the foot of the upper corner.

3. 45m 4b. Follow this to the top.

Satori 75m E2 5c

Grillo & Oddone '78

Start some way up the side entrance gully descending from the Canyon at a slab on the left, or scramble up a short chimney to the right of Il Gufo to start at the beginning of pitch 2 - more usual nowadays.

1. 25m 5b. Diagonally leftwards to a ledge and tree.

2. 25m 5b. Climb the steep wall behind the belay, then move left to belay in the easy groove line.

3. 12m 5c. Trend right across the slab to a bulging crack line. Follow this to a ledge and tree belay.

4. 13m 5b. Go diagonally right and climb the short finishing wall.

Allievi (E1 5b or HVS/AO) starts by climbing the corner further up the gully, and has one hard move passing a roof (peg) to enter the upper 5a cracks. There are two alternative second pitches to the left: **Cocaine** 5c and further left **Circo** 6a. Mostly in the

6a/b range, the Canyon itself now contains about 20 very short climbs, making it a useful retreat from excess sun or wind.

L'Anfiteatro

The natural reddish-yellow amphitheatre to the right of the canyon is similar in shape to the central wall at Malham, though the striated overhanging walls make the climbing much more thuggish. This area has seen a vast amount of development since the last guidebook - mostly in the form of short, strenuous, one-pitch routes to in-situ abseil points. An afternoon sun-trap and a good place to clock up a good E point score, or to work on a tan and watch others struggle. Most routes have the names painted in red below, and include: **Master of Bolts** 6c, **Fabiozzi Subisce Ancora** and **Rischia e Raschia** E1/HVS 5b, **Turbo Diesel** 5b, 6b has a superb alternative second pitch taking the wall between the two obvious yellow streaks - **Baci di Rio** 6b.

On the right of the overhanging wall is a rightward trending crack/pocket line:

Le Mura di Anagoor 90m E4 6b (E3 5c AO)
  Grillo & Ivaldo 1/80
1. 20m 5c. Follow the crack/pocket line right to an overhung ledge. Cross the bulge above to belay on a vague ledge.
2. 30m 5c. Follow a leftward trending line up overhanging rock by means of widely spaced but large holds to gain a slab. Follow this more delicately to a ledge and bush belay, or continue as for pitch 3.
3. 10m 4c. The slab above to another ledge.
4. 30m 6b. (5c with 2 points of aid.) Easy rock leads to the final overhangs. Pull rightwards through these to finish. (The final overhang can also be avoided by traversing right to finish as for Supervit.)

The main face to the right contains some of the classic hard routes of Finale. The juggy, pocketed wall below the main face bears several routes from 5b to 6b, all ending at a ledge. One of these would make a good alternative start to the first of these strenuous classics:

Supervit 100m E4 6a/b
  Calcagno & Grillo 6/72
A bold third pitch with well spaced bolts.
1. 20m 4b. The original start climbs the easy diagonal groove

line going up and left to the ledge.

2. 20m 6a. The impending crack line above. Belay on a ledge.

3. 30m 6a/b. Move left to an obvious easy groove line. Follow this to a huge roof, which leads extremely strenuously leftwards to belay above at a tree.

4. 30m 4b. A ramp leads easily leftwards to finish.

Stravolgimento Progressivo   45m E3 5c

Ferraresi & Parodi 9/81

Start at the foot of the easy groove of Supervit.

1. 35m 5c. Climb a vertical crack for 10m, then trend rightwards across the overhanging wall to gain a niche.

2. 10m 5c. Exit left on large sloping holds to gain the ledge above. Abseil off.

At the right-hand end of the overhanging wall, just before the arête is:

L'Ottico   90m E2 5c

Coppo, Parodi 12/79

1. 30m 5c. Overhanging pockets lead leftwards to a slab. Move up and right to more pockets, then return easily left before moving rightwards around the arête to belay in a depression.

2. 20m 5b. From the left side of the depression, climb the overhanging wall rightwards to belay in another depression.

3. 10m 5c. Exit right and make hard moves across a bulge. Move easily up the wall to a large ledge and trees.

4. 30m 5a. Trend left and make a peculiar move over a low roof to gain an easy groove line leading to the top.

Just right of the arête is the obvious corner of:

Diedro Rosso   100m HVS 5a

Titomanlio & Vaccari 5/68

Follow this in 2 pitches, trending left above the wooded ledge to finish as for L'Ottico.

Further right is the obvious pinnacle of the Campanile. Right of this is a strikingly obvious leftward flake line:

Fessura Machetto   45m E4 6b

Calcagno, Grillo & Machetto 5/72

1. 25m 6a. Starting left of the flake, climb up and right across the bulging wall to gain the flake. Follow this to less steep rock and a belay.

2. 20m 6b. Follow the flake and the hairline crack above, to a well protected but difficult finish.

(There are now a large number of short routes in the areas

around Diedro Rosso and the Campanile, with a few in the 5b/c range, most are 6a upwards with a number of 6c/7a.)

BRIC PIANARELLA

The next cliff to the south (right) of Monte Cucco is Bric Spaventaggi - characterized by the quarry on its left, and the great bulging belly (or *pancia*) in the centre - taken on the left by **Superpanza** E3 6a. Right of this is Bric Pianarella - the largest of all the cliffs of Finale. In the centre of the cliff is an obvious line of pillars - the base of these forming the lowest part of the cliff. The routes described here are to be found on the face to the left of this: the Paretone or Settore Settentrionale (Northern Sector), the centre of which has a huge eroded area of yellow rock (or *erosione*) split by the pillar of Gianni Payer. From the top of the *erosione*, a horizontal break runs left to an obvious white roof - Fivy follows a series of corners to this roof. Grimonett takes a line up the right side of the right-hand eroded area - finishing by the obvious left-right diagonal corner at the top of the cliff - and I.N.P.S. fits in between this and the line of pillars. Names are painted below some routes.

Approach
As for Monte Cucco take the Feglino road from Finale Borgo. About 100m before the turning for Orco is a small chapel on the right - park here. From the right-hand side of the chapel an obvious waymarked path leads up to the foot of the cliff - 10-15 minutes for Grimonett etc., slightly longer for Fivy.

Descent
From the top of the routes, go straight back from the cliff edge following faint paths to meet a more obvious path running parallel to the edge. Follow this leftwards (north) until a small path (blue markings) goes off to the left. Take this, and descend down old terraces into the small valley between Bric Spavantaggi and Bric Pianarella, forking left again to reach the continuation of the approach path. 20-30 minutes to return to the foot of the climbs.

Fivy   145m E2 5c (HVS 5a/A1)
   Calcagno et al 3/81
1.   15m. The easy slab diagonally rightwards past a tree to a ledge.
2.   25m 5c. (5a/A1). Up the obvious corner to a large niche.

BRIC PIANARELLA

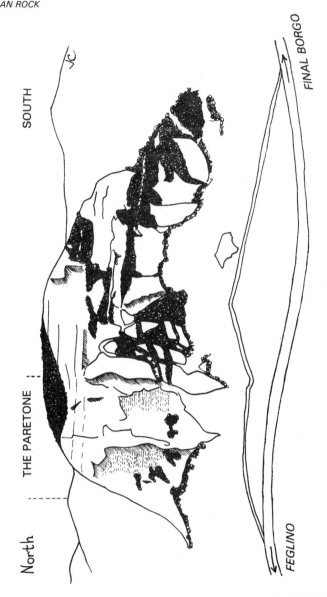

SOUTH

FINAL BORGO

THE PARETONE

North

FEGLINO

3.   30m 4b. Leave this to the right and follow a small corner to a vegetated ledge. The right-hand of the 2 small corners leads to a large ledge with trees.

4.   20m 5a. Trend diagonally rightwards to a large reddish niche. It is possible to go right here and take a fairly direct line to the top by the final 2 pitches of **Pantera Rosa**   (4b, 4a).

5.   35m 4c. Exit left and climb the wall above - first direct then diagonally leftward - to beneath the large white roof. Belay here, or traverse left for 15m to a good ledge.

6.   20m 4b. A vague corner leads up bulging rock to the final belay.

Taking a line up to the right edge of the huge yellow eroded depression is **Gianni Payer**   250m E2 5c/AO (E4 6b). Climbed free, the roof on pitch 7 is much harder than the rest of the climb. **Joe Falchetto** - the next route to the right - follows a roughly parallel line, with two 6b and two 6a pitches, it has more sustained climbing, but excellent spit protection.

For the next two routes, follow the path to the foot of the first rocks - a clean pocketed wall with red arrows pointing left. Ignore these and follow the foot of the cliff rightwards (descending steeply at first with the aid of tree roots) for about 100 metres, until an obvious earthy ramp/gully leads up diagonally rightwards.

Grimonett   250m E2 5c
Grillo & Simonetti 6/75

Towards the top of its grade; with superb rock, enjoyably exposed climbing and generally good protection this is not to be missed. A little dirty on the first 3 pitches.

Start just right of the lowest point of the face, a few metres left of the ramp/gully leading up and rightwards to the start of I.N.P.S. and Amicizia. Scramble up and left to a thin ledge and follow this leftwards to a tree belay near an obvious diagonal leftward crack - or climb the slab below to reach this direct.

1.   35m 5b. Climb the crack and the slab above to a ledge and trees. Continue up easy rock to a better tree.

2.   35m 5a. Move up a few metres to a ledge and trees below a corner. Above are the exposed roots of a tree surrounded by a mass of earth. Move right of this, climb a small slabby pillar, then move back left to the foot of an obvious flake. Climb this, traverse horizontally right, then return left to climb a groove to a stance - 2 pegs and a tree.

3.   45m 5a. Go up to the foot of a narrow corner, and climb this

BRIC PIANARELLA -
THE PARETONE

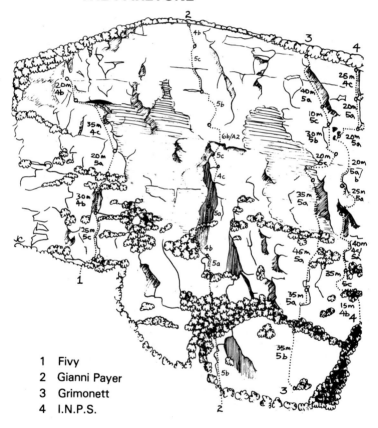

1 Fivy
2 Gianni Payer
3 Grimonett
4 I.N.P.S.

to a ledge and trees (possible stance). Go up into an open corner and cross a delicate wall diagonally rightwards, until easier angled rock leads to a belay beneath yellow eroded rock. (The delicate rightward traverse can be avoided below.)

4. 35m 5a. Up a corner, then climb overhanging rock - first direct, then leftwards to a niche below threads (possible belay). Pull over the overhang and move left to belay on two pegs and a bolt. An amazing pitch amongst superb rock architecture.

5. 20m 5c. Exit leftwards, climb a wall, then traverse easily right to beneath a roof. Over this to another niche.

6. 30m 5b. Exit left, return right by a wall, and follow a corner and short wall past a tree to a ledge.

7. 10m 5c. A corner leads delicately left to a ledge.

8. 40m 5a. The original route finished diagonally rightwards, but the usual (and better) finish is to follow an open corner leading left to beneath a line of overhangs. Move rightwards over these, and go up to the summit.

I.N.P.S.   200m E2 5c (HVS/E1 5a/AO)
   Leardi et al 1/80
Right of Grimonett a vegetated ramp line leads up rightwards. Scramble up the earthy ramp/gully right of Grimonett to tree belays near its top. An obvious groove slants up from right to left with I.N.P.S. painted at its foot. Less sustained than Grimonett, most of the climbing is HVS in standard, and the use of a few points of aid on the second pitch would reduce the grade to an enjoyable HVS/E1.

1. 15m 4b. Climb steeply up to the left to gain an easy slabby groove and follow this leftwards over ledges to an earth ledge below a steep wall.

2. 35m 5c. Follow a steep crack leftwards to a slab. Climb this with a difficult move rightwards around a rib, and continue up to a good tree belay.

3. 40m 4c/5a. Move rightwards (awkward move to start), then climb diagonally rightwards and up to a ledge below the *erosione*. Steep rock leads to the foot of a corner - climb this passing a huge crystal thread to a stance in an Alladin's Cave of crystals. An amazing pitch.

4. 25m 5a. Exit right, climb direct, then move left to a stance with threads in a small cave.

5. 20m 5a/b. Exit right and follow pegs delicately rightwards to another cave.

6. 20m 5a. Exit right and go up to a hole. Layback up into this

and continue trending rightwards to an earth ledge. Follow this rightwards for about 8 metres to a large tree.

7.   20m 5a. Climb the crack above the tree - many pegs - and continue up to trees.

8.   25m 4c. Climb the easy groove to the top.

Best started as for I.N.P.S. to avoid the normal aided first pitch,

L'Amicizia takes a line to the right of that route. The overhanging wall of the last pitch but one is 6a free, and is best avoided by traversing left to the stance of I.N.P.S. and finishing up its last two pitches. This gives a good classic HVS climb.

ROCCA DI PERTI

Fifteen hundred metres in length and up to a hundred and fifty in height, Rocca di Perti is more a group of crags than a single entity, making it a particularly good choice for bank holidays and other busy periods. Generally facing south, it is one of the best venues for the cooler months, although it is possible to find shady climbs on the northern sector. There is an excellent range of routes for the middle grade climber as just over half of the fifty-odd climbs in the '83 guide were graded HVS or below, although more recent developments have ensured there is ample choice in the higher grades.

The rather neglected extreme left-hand section of the main cliff (Settore Settentrionale) contains routes of up to 150 metres (mostly in the VS/HVS range, plus a V.Diff., a Severe and a number of harder routes including Mariacher's **Spit Surf**, the hardest climb in the old '83 guide. The north ridge itself is an interesting scramble. The rest of Perti's climbs are predominantly of one or two pitches, and on some of the roughest rock in Finale - it's no accident that there's a route called La Grattugia - The Grater!

Approach

1.   About 3.5m from Final Borgo the Calice road passes under the autostrada. Take the second turning on the right after this, and follow the narrow road until it passes back under the motorway through a low tunnel. Park just after this and follow the track round several hairpins to the foot of the crag - 15 minutes. The initial steep section of this track has been so badly eroded by climbers' cars that it is now virtually impassable for normal vehicles.

ROCCA DI PERTI

1 Parete delle Gemme
2 Settore delle Ombre Blu
3 Settore Meridionale (South)
4 Settore Settentrionale (North)
5 Settore Centrale

2. Take the Calice road as above, but this time take the turning on the right before the autostrada - signposted 'Perti'. Drive through the village of Perti and continue behind the ridge to a small parking area at the end of the road - about two and a half miles from the Calice road. This is particularly useful for routes on the Settore Settentrionale. As local people have fenced-off meadows previously used for parking there is now only room for about 10 vehicles in this area - adequate for mid-week climbing, but strictly for early birds at weekends.

The Parete delle Gemme

Right next to the track, and when using the first approach the first crag to be encountered, is this popular lower tier with its fine crop of short E1s and HVSs, as well as some more recent eliminates. As it is particularly useful for either a warm-up or that one last route, at weekends it tends to be crowded early and late in the day. To the right is an area of black stalactites, and on the left of the obvious smooth tower of:

Pilastrino   45m E1 5b/E2 5c

Grillo & Oddone 1/80

1. 30m 5b. Precarious climbing leads up the left side of the rounded pillar to a break (becoming polished). Exit either left, or direct - harder and poorly protected. Finish here or:

2. 15m 5c. The steep little wall behind - worthwhile. (This is actually the top pitch of Schifinix, which takes the wall left of Pilastrino at 6a.)

The wall to the right is taken by:

I Germogli   50m VS 4c

Grillo & Oddone 1/80

1. 30m 4c. Starting just left of the toe of the buttress, climb the wall to a tree.

2. 20m 4c. The open crack above. The crack to the right - Fessura della Sperimentazione - provides a slightly harder finish (5a nuts required), whilst the slab to the left is Cric e Croc 5b.

Further right is a diagonal ramp running up from right to left. A corner crack goes up from the highest point of the ramp to an obvious roof (**Fessura Convalescent**   5a).

O Palliano   45m E2 5c

Grillo & Ivaldo 2/82

1. 20m 5c. Starting from the ramp just right of the crack, climb

the bulging wall to a stance on the ledge.
 Abseil off, or:
2.   20m 6a/b. **Tetto del Kaiser**.
 Move left and climb the crack to the roof. Follow this rightwards until it is possible to pull over the overhang and climb the wall above.

 Just right along the ramp, with a bulging start is **Dramma al Cibali/Adrenaline** (6a, 5b/c), and right of this is:

Le Sacrifice   40m HVS 5a/b
 Grillo & Ivaldo 12/82
1.   20m 5a. Traverse right from the ramp and move up the wall to a ledge - belay here or continue by:
2.   20m 5a/b. Climb the overhanging wall on huge holds.

Via di Walter   45m HVS 5a
 Savio et al 6/80
Start below the stalactites.
1.   45m 5a. Move leftwards across the slab to a small ledge (stance and belay pegs). Climb the leaning groove, moving slightly right to finish, or continue direct - slightly harder.

Flebo   40m E1 5b/c
 Manfredini & Parodi 12/81
Start as for Walter.
1.   Climb straight up to the stalactites and move left through the bulges on good holds. Move up an awkward slab to exit right around the roof (or finish slightly leftwards).
Descent
Follow a path to the right (facing in).
 N.B. At the same level but well to the right (below the Settore Meridionale) is the Placca dell'Oasi. Developed in 1986, this now boasts about 10 single pitch routes of 20/30 metres. Mostly in the 5b/6a range, but with two VS/HVSs, all the routes are said to be worthwhile.

Settore delle Ombre Blu

The next buttress to the right. Continue up the track past two bends to a barrier, from where a faint path leads up left to the foot of the crag. Near the left arête is an obvious area of eroded yellow rock - the corner crack above giving the line of Oddonett. To the right, and close to the foot of the rock is a large tree with exposed roots. Ombre Blu starts by a faint crack just left of this tree, with the open corner groove above supplying the substance of the route.

Oddonett   30m HVS 5a
Oddone & Simonetti '79

An excellent pitch in its own right, and a good warm-up for the harder climbs.

Starting just right of the cave, climb easily rightwards to the foot of the corner. Climb this to the top. Either abseil off from the chains to the left of the stance (as for Lo Diceva etc.) or continue by two more pitches of 4b and 5a.

Three other short pitches start as for Oddonett. To the left is **Freestyle** (5c), whereas starting from the top of the easy rock below the corner to climb the left and right arêtes of this are respectively: **Lo Diceva Neruda** etc. and **Menhir** (both 5b/c).

Ombre Blu   60m E2 5c
Ivaldo & Grillo 1/80

1.   30m 5b/c. After a hard start up the bulging wall left of the faint crack, enjoyable HVS climbing leads leftwards to the foot of the groove-line, then diagonally right to belay on a ledge below a large hole.

2. 30m 5c. Diagonally leftwards to a small tree in the groove, then back right to a good thread. Return to the groove and climb this with sustained interest - crux below the small roof. Belay at a tree on the large ledge.

From here it is possible to move slightly left and climb another 30m pitch just left of a small arête (5a). Most prefer to abseil from chains to the right (facing in).

Gridonett   30m E1/2 5b
Grillo, Oddone & Simonetti '79

An alternative second pitch to Ombre Blu, avoiding the corner groove by moving right from the first stance, returning left to belay as above.

Several metres to the right is a cave some way above the ground. Scramble rightwards over the tree roots and down to a point just right of this. The next two climbs have their names painted below.

Ci Mande Nicone   25m E3 6a
L.Castiglia 4/85

A superbly sustained and varied climb.

From the start of Pertuccia move diagonally leftwards to the foot of the cave and climb the pillar forming its left wall. Overcome the roof (crux) and climb the sustained slab above, moving right at the top to belay as for Pertuccia.

La Pertuccia 25m E3 5c (35m E4 6a)
   Castiglia 4/85
1.   25m 5c. Steep, sustained pocket climbing following a line of pegs up the rounded pillar to the right.
   It is usual to abseil from here - thus avoiding the awkward little second pitch!
2.   10m 6a. Move up to the short bulging wall above - climb this by its right arête - sharp rock!
   The line just right is newer than the '87 guidebook and is slightly easier than Pertuccia (E2 5c).

   The following climbs lie to the left of Oddonett. The foot of the cliff now falls back behind thick vegetation. Fifty metres left of Oddonett is a steep wall with a small vegetated pillar/ramp on the right. Starting 6m up this is:
Allegro Ma Non Troppo 30m E3 5c
   Bausone et al 3/82
1.   30m 5c. Trend leftwards across the slabby wall to a cave. Move left and climb a steeper section direct, move left again then return right to finish. Abseil off.
   Vacca Treno (5c) and **Saltipicchio** (6b) are variations on Allegro, the former taking a direct line via the left end of the cave, the latter starting further left.

   Left again is an eroded area of impending reddish rock. The gently overhanging finger-crack with a difficult exit is **Sublimizione** (20m 6b), whereas the wall on the right is a Finale test-piece: **Mamy Avvista** 7a (Mami on Sight).

   By scrambling up and leftwards through the trees one comes to another vegetated pillar with a disgustingly muddy cleft on its left-hand side. Despite its uninviting appearance, the short speleologic-al scramble is worthwhile to reach the foot of the superb:
Muro del Pianto (The Wailing Wall) 90m E2 5b
   Belmonte & Leardi 4/82
1.   30m 5b. Climb the thin crack, making a hard move to pass a peg. Easier climbing leads diagonally leftwards past an overlap to a ledge.
2.   30m 5b. Move up to the overhang, overcome this to the left and continue to a ledge.
3.   30m 5b. Traverse right and climb up into a cave. From the top

of this make an exposed traverse leftwards to a groove. Climb this to the top.

Left of the muddy cleft are two short pitches which can be used as variant starts to the above. The first is **Quo Vadis** (15m 5c and said to be excellent), slightly further left is **Freezer** (5b). A suitable continuation to one of these would be **Resol Riama** (50m 6a, 5c) - the wall to the left of pitch 2 of Muro del Pianto, easily reached by walking along the ledge from the first stance.

Settore Meridionale
(Southern Sector)

The area above and right of Ombre Blu. The track continues to the right, eventually curving back left to pass directly beneath the rock. Follow the track for about 200m to where a path cuts up the hillside to rejoin the upper section of the track below a superb 50m wall with a vegetated corner on its right. The wall is taken by the magnificent Mario Piotti and the climbs are described moving left from this.

Descent
Walk left (north) and follow the track to the foot of the climbs.

Mario Piotti   45m E2 5c/6a
   Calcagno, Grillo and Oliva 12/81
Scramble through vegetation to start at the right of the wall.
1.   20m 5b. A shallow groove trends leftwards, follow this until it is possible to move left around the arête onto a slab. Move up then back right to an obvious belay on a small ledge almost directly above the start.
2.   20m 5c/6a. Fairly straightforward, but poorly protected climbing leads past a peg to a fault line. Traverse left along this and make a hard move to gain the start of a vague crack line. Follow this to the obvious stance on the left arête.

It is possible to abseil from here, but unless the poor in-situ tat (late October '87) has been replaced by chains, it is better to continue by:
3.   5m 4b. Easily up, then right to trees on a ledge - abseil from these.

A variant pitch 2 with well-spaced bolts - **Lupi dell'Ontario**   6a - climbs almost directly to these trees, whereas **Panierino, Banane e ce ne Fosse** (40m 6c, 6a) climbs more or less direct from the groove of Piotti to the first stance, before continuing up the wall right of Lupi dell'Ontario.

A serious, and strenuous route with well-spaced bolts starts behind the tree left of Mario Piotti:

Mazz Art   35m E5 6b
1.   20m 6a. Move left over a bulging start, and continue leftwards across the slab to a bolt belay.
2.   15m 6b. Climb the steep wall left of the first stance of Mario Piotti to the second belay of that route.

Some way to the left is an obvious pillar with a large vegetated gully on its left. Starting 10m right of this at a detached flake is:

Florivana   60m VS 4c
  Carlini & Mesciulam '74
1.   30m 4c. Climb up to and around the flake, and move right to a tree. Climb a short corner and traverse diagonally right to a stance on a good ledge below a corner.
2.   30m 4c. Climb the corner until it narrows, and make a diagonal traverse rightwards to bushes and trees.
3.   10m. Easily to the top.

Go-Go   E4 6a/b
  Grillo & Oddone 1/79   FFA P.Gomersall
Start as for Florivana.
1.   20m 6a. Climb directly up to a leftward leaning groove crack. Follow this over a bulge to belay on the slab above. (Hexes 7/8 required.)
2.   10m 6b. Climb the innocuous-looking finger-crack through several bulges - good value!

The pillar itself gives the strenuous:

Pilier della Concentrazione   60m E2/3 5c
  Grassi & Mesciulam 11/74
A vegetated crack runs up from near the toe of the pillar.
1.   30m 5c. Climb the crack - or better the face on the right - and go up to the foot of the overhanging crack. Struggle up this past several pegs, and move left to a stance overlooking the gully.
2.   30m 5b. Move right and gain the top of a large unstable block. The off-width above is well protected by Friends and bolts on its right wall, and gives pleasant climbing.

Left of the Pilier is a large yellow-red erosion cave, several metres above the ground. The next climb starts below this.

Il Tamburo   40m HVS 5a/b
  Coppo & Ramondini '78

1.   Climb up to the cave and exit right. Move up the slab and either trend right up easier rock to the top, or climb the right side of the pillar (delicate) to gain the R side of the upper cave. Abseil off.

Danza Saracena   50m E2 5c
1.   5b. As for Tamburo to belay in the cave.
2.   5c. From the left edge of the upper cave traverse horizontally left for several metres and climb the obvious overhanging crack past a peg. (The roof above the cave is **La Strega** - 7b?)

Left of the cave, another pillar forms the last obvious feature before the top of the track. This is:

Pilastrino Marantonio   32m E3 6a
     Marantonio et al
1.   12m 5c. Climb the slightly overhanging scoop just right of the arête. Belay below the pillar, or continue by:
2.   20m 6a. Follow the crack line up the pillar, moving first right, then left at the top.

The crack/groove to the left is **L'Isola Che Non C'e** (30m HVS 4c/5a) which can also be used as an easier, but inferior start, and the wall between this and the Pilastro is **I Nuovi Guerri**   6c.

Settore Settentrionale
(Northern Sector)

Approach
Either: (1) From the barrier across the track above the Parete delle Gemme; take the track through the woods passing between the Parete and the Settore Ombre Blu. At a fork turn left and descend to reach the foot of the Settore (continuing upwards by the right fork brings you to the Settore Centrale).

Or: (2) Go west from the top car park and descend to a small col below the North Ridge - a good place to leave sacs. Follow the path which descends to a point below two large yellow caves in the face above. To the right is an obvious groove line, with an overhanging wall to the right of this. Just left of the groove is a slim pillar.

E.T.   40m E3 5c
     Grillo & Oliva 3/83
1.   40m 5c. Follow the obvious line up the pillar, trending right to belay at trees in a vegetated funnel above the central groove. Abseil off.

Spit Surf   40m E5 6b
   Mariacher & Jovine 4/83
A serious route, protected first by small nuts and in-situ pegs and threads, then by widely spaced bolts.
1.   20m 6a. Strenuously up the centre of the overhanging wall right of E.T. by a vague line to a hanging belay.
2.   20m 6b. Zig-zag up the steep wall - 2 bolts off to the side. Abseil off.

   The climbs to the left and right of those described above, are some of the longest at Perti, and would seem worthy of investigation by the VS/HVS leader. Particularly recommended is **Antica Osteria**   80m HVS 5a/b.

   About 100m to the right is the Settore Centrale. The massive groove line at the top of the crag is taken by:
Luisella   75m E1 5b (HVS 4c/5a/AO)
Scramble up easy rock to the toe of a blunt pillar.
1.   35m 5b. (4c/5a AO). Climb the pillar, first trending left to pass an awkward bulge, then direct, until it is possible to traverse right to belay at a vegetated ledge.
2.   40m 5a. Follow the initial groove line to the base of the main corner. Climb its right wall to the top. (The grey pillar to the left of the corner is **Belin, Statique, Je Suis Content**   20m 6b, and the wall to the right **Alba di Giada**   20m 6b.)
Descent
Either, follow the crest of the ridge north, and scramble down to return to the col mentioned in the second approach above. Or, follow the crest rightwards (south) to reach the large track which passes beneath the Settore Meridionale (Mario Piotti etc.).

MONTESORDO
(The SW part of Rocca Carpanea)
Approach
One of the less popular crags of the area, Montesordo is the cliff clearly visible to the SE of the parking area described in the second approach to Rocca di Perti. From the parking area a track (signposted to caves) leads NE and curves round through a small hamlet before continuing downhill to the SE. The main path soon bears off left to the caves. Ignore this and continue downhill (south) along a narrow path until a smaller path turns left up to the crag - arriving below the main face (Settore Centrale) which contains the routes

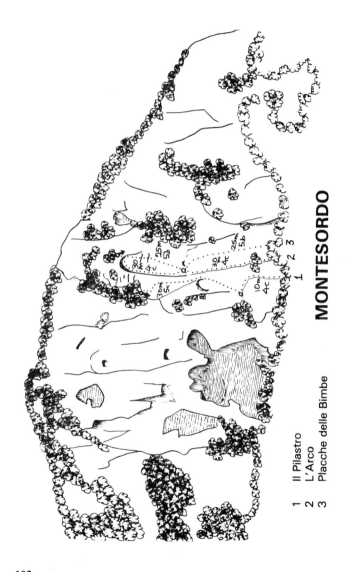

MONTESORDO

1 Il Pilastro
2 L'Arco
3 Placche delle Bimbe

described here. The cliff is always visible until it disappears behind trees near the final approach path, which was partly obscured by felled trees in '85/86. Another approach leads from the roadside parking places lower down the road via the dog-kennels to a house, and then turns uphill to the cliff - not for the faint-hearted! 15/20 minutes.

Settore Centrale

About 80m in height, it is characterized by a large cave/depression at the foot of the left-hand side of the face. Above this is an overhanging wall, and to the right an obvious pillar about two-thirds the height of the face. This is taken by Il Pilastro. The very obvious rightward curving corner crack to the right is followed by L'Arco, and Bimbe climbs the curving slab to the right of this.

As escape from the top of all routes is both difficult and unpleasant, descents should be made by abseil from fixed points.

Il Pilastro (Franco & Ketty)   45m E2 4c, 5c
Leardi & Parodi 3/81
Start at the right side of the small subsidiary pillar below the left arête of the pillar.
1.   25m 4c. Climb to the top of the small pillar and continue to a stance on the left arête of the main pillar.
2.   20m 5c. Trend rightwards across the pillar, and move right across the bulge. Move up to a choice of finishes to reach the top of the pillar - none of which are easy. Abseil off.

Introspezione Elettrostatica   40m E3 5c
M.Frigo 1986
Starting just to the right, this direct on Il Pilastro gives a superbly sustained pitch. Either join the above at the bulge, or finish up the arête to the right. Can be split at chains level with Il Pilastro, but this is somewhat of a cop-out.

L'Arco   60m VS 4c
Calcagno & Grillo 6/73
One of the best of the easier Finale classics.
1.   30m 4c. The corner leads slightly rightwards to a tree, and widens above. Jamming, then bridging lead to a stance with pegs to the right of the crack.
2.   30m 4c. Climb the face above the stance to rejoin the crack. Follow this enjoyably rightward below the arch which gives it its name. Abseil from tree.

Placche delle Bimbe   50m E2 5b
   Grillo & Marantonio 12/80
1.   25m 5b. Climb the steep bulging wall right of L'Arco to gain
the slab above. Move slightly left to belay as for L'Arco.
2.   25m 5b. Climb the slab trending diagonally rightwards. Abseil
off. (Can be climbed in one long pitch.)

Lo Specchio

This is the rightward continuation of the Settore Centrale, reached
by walking about a hundred metres rightwards and descending to
the foot of the cliff. Most of the climbs are excellently protected by
spits. The main pitch of the first climb - **Super Bostick** (30m HVS
5a) - can be reached by scrambling upwards instead of down.
After a strenuous start on huge pockets, the upper slab is unfortunately rather dirty, with spaced protection.

L'Alveare (The Beehive)

Well to the left of the Settore Centrale, this area of bulging
pocketed rocks boasts some of Finale's most difficult problems,
including **Viaggio nel Futuro**   7c+, **Diverso Peverso**   7b, and the
area's first 8b, **Hyaena** (all French grades).

ROCCA DI CORNO

A great tooth of grey and yellow limestone bursting through its
hilltop vegetation, Corno has some of the best climbing in Finale.
This ranges from the superb extremes of the pocketed South Wall
to a pair of good VSs on the smaller SE face - not forgetting Ipsilon,
one of the best limestone HVSs anywhere. An excellent venue for
the cooler months of the year - including winter - it can also provide
a sheltered haven from strong winds.

Approach
Drive north from Finale Pia through Calvisio. About half a mile after
the village a turning to the right leads over a bridge to a series of
hairpin bends - Corno is clearly visible on the left. (It is also possible
to reach this point by a twisting narrow road from Monte Cucco via
Orco, Boragni and Ponte Cornei - about 4 miles.) An obvious track
leads off left from the last and tightest bend to beneath the crag.

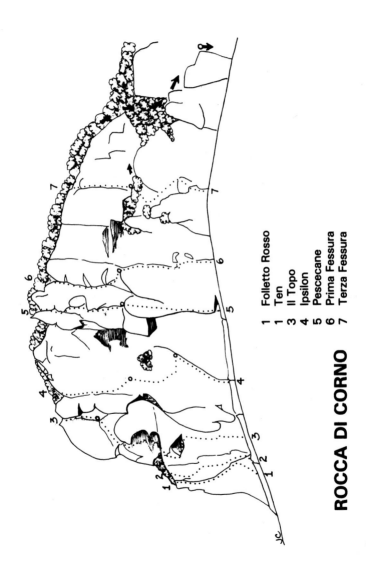

ROCCA DI CORNO

1 Folletto Rosso
1 Ten
3 Il Topo
4 Ipsilon
5 Pescecane
6 Prima Fessura
7 Terza Fessura

105

At peak weekends such as Easter, it may be best to park at the bend and walk along the track, this adds no more than five minutes to the approach. A path leads steeply up the hillside from a Roman bridge, arriving near the foot of the pillar of Pescecane (ten minutes). Walk left below the S. Wall to arrive at the diagonal corner of Folletto Rosso, the climbs are described moving left from here.

Descent
For routes on the main S. Wall, follow a path off to the right (facing in). Continuing in the same direction, scramble down diagonally rightwards to a ledge and follow this for a short distance to where a short (15/20m) abseil leads over a rock step to the foot of the cliff.

The South Wall

The face is split by a horizontal ledge at roughly half-height. Above this the rock becomes more broken, and the majority of climbs finish at the ledge. The lower face is defined on the left by an obvious diagonal corner crack going up to the left. This is the line of:

Folletto Rosso   30m E2 6a
   Leardi & Parodi 11/77
Start on a ledge with trees, several metres above the base of the crag to the left of the crack line. Most of the climbing is at 5b, with one much harder but well protected move. Abseil from the ledge.

   Right of this, about 5m above the ground, is a niche with twin vertical cracks leading upwards.

Ten   30m E2 5c
   Calcagno, Grillo, Ivaldo 1/82
A wonderful pitch following a natural line - abseil off.

   Several metres right, and starting from a ledge is:

Due Dita di Violenza   30m E3 6a
   Ferraresi & Parodi 12/82
With a fierce undercut start, this takes a line between Ten and the less sustained:

Il Topo   80m E2 6a
   Piotti et al 2/72
1.   40m 5b. A thin crack gives enjoyable climbing to a cave.
2.   40m 6a. Move up rightwards to another cave, then back left

to enter a strenuous crack. Climb this with a hard move into wide bridging.

Ipsilon 50m HVS 5a
   Titomanlio (to ledge), Mesciulam (the corner) '74
Start at the foot of a corner crack that forms a 'Y' above, below the left edge of a large cave. Well protected.
1.   10m. The corner leads past a tree to a belay below the cave.
2.   15m 5a. Traverse delicately leftwards past several pegs to the crack forming the left branch of the 'Y'. Climb this and the slab above to the large ledge. (Odeon 6a, climbs the wall below to reach this point more or less directly.)
3.   30m 5a. The superb corner above.

A number of new routes have been climbed between Folletto Rosso and Ipsilon. With their names painted below, they are:
Alchemie d'Estate 6a, **Proiettile Umano** E2 6a, **Bei Tempi** 6a, **Destine Anime** E5 6b, **Fora et Labora** 6b, and **Sylvester** 6c (just right of Ipsilon).

Some metres to the right is a huge cave-like recess, topped by a large roof. Right of this is an obvious rounded pillar with an undercut base. This divides the South Wall from the SE Face and is taken by:
Pescecane 30m E3/4 6a/b
   E. & G.L.Vaccari 5/72
A small, but obvious niche can be seen at about ten metres, the direct line by the crack to the right is 6b, moving left makes it somewhat easier. After a short 5a section, a second pitch continues easily to the top.

(Immediately right is **La Signora in Rosso** 6a/b.)

The S.E.Face

Three good middle-grade routes have been saddled with very pedestrian names. The first starts up the rightward facing corner to the right of Pescecane:

Prima Fessura 60m VS 4c
   Benassi et al 11/72
1.   30m 4c. Climb the corner past a difficult undercut start.
2.   30m 4b. The pleasant corner on the left needs nuts for protection. (The right-hand crack is a strenuous 5b.)
   Moving right, the second crack is a 40m Severe, and the third

has a particularly good first pitch - much better than it looks.

Terza Fessura   50m VS 4c
  Benassi & Grillo 11/72

1.   40m 4c. Steep moves lead to enjoyable bridging past several pegs. Walk off right or continue by another pitch of a similar standard.

   Note: Some way to the left of Folletto Rosso is the West Face with its interesting rock architecture. The first buttress has a trio of worthwhile middle-grade climbs; **Il Muro Crepitante** E1 5b (protected by small nuts and threads), **Bettabel** E1 5b, and **Massimiliano Ferretti**   HVS 5a.

MUZZERONE (La Spezia)

A hundred and fifty kilometres along the coast to the east of Genoa is the natural harbour of La Spezia. Between here and Levanto, some 25km to the west, is the beautiful area of coastal scenery, pine forests and picturesque villages known as the Cinque Terre - with its extensive network of waymarked trails, a paradise for walkers. The seaward cliffs of the headland forming the western side of the gulf of La Spezia are known as Muzzerone. Composed of a superb marbled limestone, in the 1980's they have been rapidly developed by a small but talented group of local climbers, particularly Davide Battistella and Roberto Vigiani.

The cliffs begin at Portovenere, but although there is some climbing here (including a traverse 10m above the sea), it is the beaches and narrow shopping streets of this ancient fishing/tourist village that hold most interest. From here the cliffs rise to form a discontinuous series of white walls and pillars rising up to 300m above the sea, often topped by decaying bunkers and other remains of wartime fortifications. These provide useful landmarks when locating the different areas. Nine areas have been developed as yet, but the potential is enormous - not least on the sheer walls of the islands, although access is somewhat difficult!

Facing between south and south-west, climbing is possible throughout the year, though restricted to mornings and evenings in the hottest months. With its easy motorway access, a few days at Muzzerone would provide an excellent contrast to Finale as the climbing is very different in character. The routes on the Parete Striata are particularly recommended - their length, and remote position high above the sea making them memorable experiences.

Davide Battistella is preparing an Italian guidebook to the area, and has supplied the bulk of the information in this section. 'E' grades have been given only to the small number of routes I have climbed here, and it is likely that the technical grades on other routes will be somewhat harsher than their equivalents at, for example, Finale.

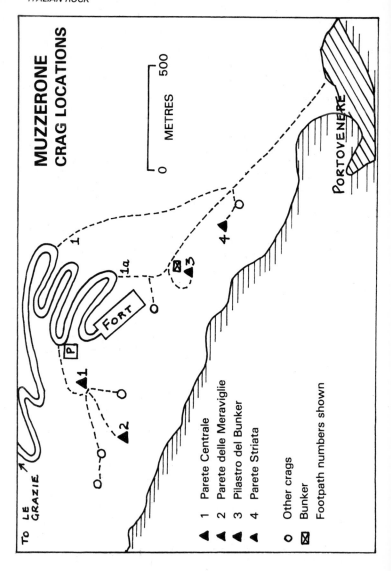

MUZZERONE CRAG LOCATIONS

To LE GRAZIE

1 Parete Centrale
2 Parete delle Meraviglie
3 Pilastro del Bunker
4 Parete Striata

○ Other crags
⊠ Bunker
   Footpath numbers shown

FORT

PORTOVENERE

METRES

0   500

Approach

To La Spezia by various autostrade, eg. along the coast from Genoa, or from Milan and the north via Piacenza and Parma. From La Spezia take the Portovenere road until a turning to the right signposted 'il Monte Castellane', just before the village of La Grazie. After about 5km take a fork to the left (the M. Castellane road continuing to the right). Carry on past several hairpin bends to another fork. Keep always left and this soon brings you to an obvious parking place distinguished by a low rock wall with a mountain rescue plaque (Soccorso Alpino) high up on the left, and a track leading through a break in the rock to the right. For the Parete Centrale walk through the gap and turn left down large rock steps leading under the wall to its foot.

It should perhaps be mentioned that the scenery of abandoned quarries on either side of the steep road up from La Grazie, is somewhat less than inspiring, with the smoke pouring forth from the cratered top of Monte Castellane making a passable film-set for Tolkien's Mordor. However, once on the cliffs the atmosphere completely changes, and all this seems a world away.

Camping etc.

To stay at the (expensive) campsite near Portovenere it is necessary to book well in advance, but it is possible to camp in the area below the Central Wall (water available from the fountain in La Grazie where you turn off the Portovenere road). A rifugio at nearby Campiglia is due to open in December '87.

The Parete Centrale
(Central Wall)

About 100m long and 50m high, with easy access, excellent rock, and a fine collection of short, well protected climbs (bolts and pegs), this is the most popular area at Muzzerone. The climbing is steeper (and harder) than it looks, and often relies on the use of tiny 'ears' of rock. Seemingly fragile on first acquaintance, these are actually very solid, although the roughness of the rock is less than kind to finger-tips. Although those listed below are all in the E2-E5 range, there are several easier and worthwhile climbs from V.Diff. upwards taking obvious natural lines on the right-hand section of the face. Many routes have names painted below. The route numbers refer to the diagrams on pages 112 and 113.

**MUZZERONE
PARETE CENTRALE**

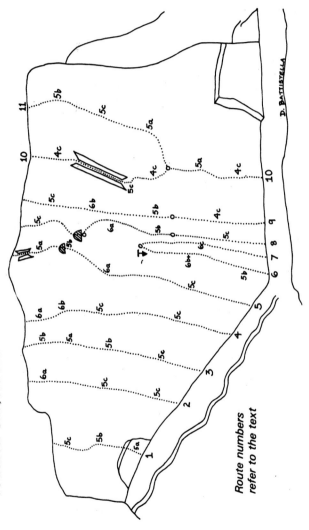

*Route numbers
refer to the text*

MUZZERONE PARETE CENTRALE Right hand sector

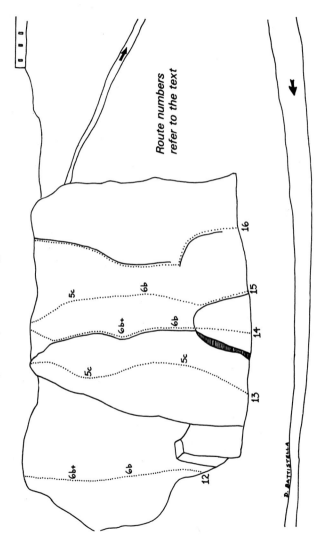

Route numbers refer to the text

From left to right the routes are:
1. **Trappola per Topi** (Battistella)   25m 5c.
2. **As Fidanken** (Battistella)   30m 6a.
3. **Flipper** (Vigiani)   35m 5c.
4. **Gonna Fly Now** (Vigiani)   35m 6b.
5. **Torna a Casa Lessi** (Vigiani)   40m 6a.
6. **Stratagoing** (Di Bono)   25m 6b +.
7. **Mami on Sight** (Battistella)   25m 6c.
8. **Brutta Fasenda**(Di Bono)   40m 6a (E3).
9. **Punzuli e Lamelle** (Vigiani)   45m 6b.
10. **Via Lidia** (Battistella)   45m 5c (E2).
11. **Spit and Span** (Battistella)   25m 5c.

Right-hand Sector
12. **Delicatessen** (Battistella)   20m 6b +.
13. **Rimba** (Battistella)   25m 5c.
14. **Lo Spigolino** (Vigiani)   25m 6b +.
15. **Vavumba** (Vigiani)   25m 6b.
16. **Handy Grip** (Vigiani)   25m 6b.

In the autumn of '87, Davide Battistella succeeded on Banzai. At French 7c+ (English 7a) this is now the hardest route on both the Parete Centrale and Muzzerone as a whole.

Parete delle Meraviglie
(The Wall of Wonders)

Access

From the base of the central wall, follow a constructed path leftwards (facing the sea). Walk along the top of a stone wall and descend its left end. Descend a gully directly towards the sea to reach an obvious ledge on the left, which divides the main cliff from a subsidiary one. The routes start here - ten minutes. (Two easy routes start in the gully just above, the obvious line of pegs being **Via Donne** VS.) As well as the routes listed here, there are now a number of new routes in this area. Particularly recommended are the Spigolo and Excalibur - both have their names painted below.

Route numbers refer to the diagram on page 115.

MUZZERONE
PARETE DELLE MERAVIGLIE

*Route numbers
refer to the text*

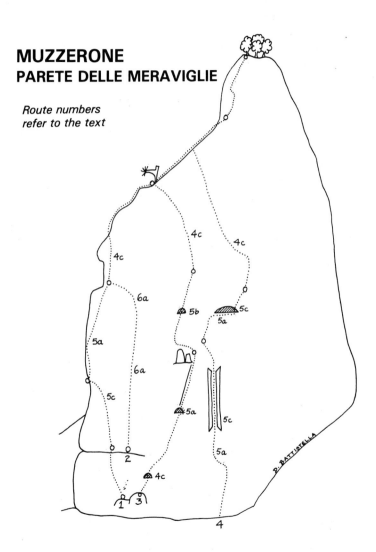

From the left the routes are:

1. **Spigolo delle Meraviglie** (Vigiani & Castagna)   120m 5c.
2. **Muro di Fuoco** (Battistella & Di Bono)   45m 6a.
3. **Excalibur** (Battistella & Di Bono)   70m HVS/E1 5b.
4. **Morning Dream** (Vigiani & Battistella)   80m 5c.

Pilastro del Bunker

In a glorious position at the NW end of the Parete Striata, this imposing 200m high pillar bears one of the classics of Muzzerone.

Access

Park at the next hairpin after the parking area for the Parete Centrale (i.e. below and left of a large fort where the road ends). Follow the marked path (Sentiero 1a to Portovenere) northwards to a bunker on the crest of the ridge. Descend the gully below this to its end. Looking out towards the sea, a small path leads off to the left. Follow this to a large pine tree at the beginning of the route. 15 minutes.

Chi Vuol Esser Lieto Sia   200m 5a/b
Vigiani & Amore

1. 40m 5a/b. Traverse a few metres rightwards around the edge of the pillar. Climb a yellowish crack to its end, traverse right across a slab to another crack, and follow this to a belay.
2. 40m 4a. Follow the crack above, then the arête.
3. 35m 5a. Superb climbing up a slab followed by a crack. Starting with a short friable section, traverse right to another stance.
4. 40m 5a. Direct over excellent rock for a few metres, until a crack leads rightwards via a cleft to a stance.
5. 30m. Trend easily leftwards to a large tree at the foot of the final pitch.
6. 35m 5a. A beautiful juggy slab leads to a crack on the left. Follow this and a series of slabs to exit at the top of the pillar.

The Parete Striata
(Striped Wall)

Undoubtedly the most wild and beautiful area, this superb wall extends for approximately 500m in width, reaches 200m in height, and contains some of the best routes of Muzzerone. The

MUZZERONE PARETE STRIATA

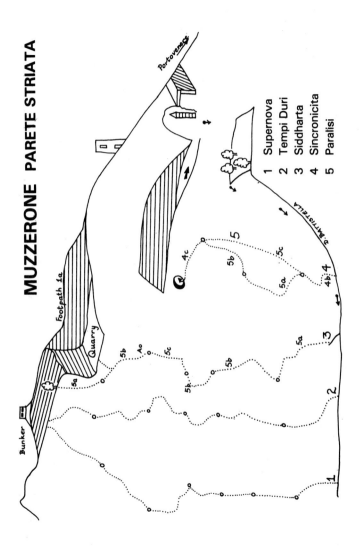

1 Supernova
2 Tempi Duri
3 Siddharta
4 Sincronicità
5 Paralisi

situations are like nothing else to be found in this guidebook, and the climbs have an atmosphere all of their own, with a feeling of remoteness somewhat similar to some routes on Gogarth or the Ormes. As the foot of the face is about a hundred metres above the sea, the routes are accessible at all times.

The wall is composed of sheets of extremely hard marble/limestone in sloping horizontal bands of white and grey-black - thus the name Parete Striata. On first sight it appears to be very broken by ledges and trees, but although these provide excellent belays the actual climbs are surprisingly continuous, and only on closer contact do you discover the softer yellow sections of rock weathered into roofs and overhangs which often form the crux sections of climbs.

Access

As for Pilastro Del Bunker, but trending left before the bunker to descend steeply past another abandoned building. Continue towards Portovenere for approx. 50m and then go right (seawards), to arrive on the flat concrete roof of another small bunker. Descend a short steel ladder (painted green) over the seaward edge of the bunker to a ledge, follow this to the right and descend a path then fixed ropes over easy ground (first left then back right) to arrive at a large terrace with a naturally polished marble floor. From here there is a superb view of the great striped wall, and the coast of the Cinque Terre beyond.

Fixed ropes lead to the base of the wall, and then across this to reach the foot of Supernova on the extreme left of the wall (this and all subsequent directions are given facing into the cliff). Name painted on the rock.

Route numbers refer to the diagram on page 117.

1. **Supernova**   200m E3 5c/6a. (2 points of aid) E4 6b free
   Manicardi & Di Bono

A stupendous route, mostly on perfect rock. Fully equipped with pegs, bolts and chained stances, carry a few small to medium wires.

1.   30m 4b/c. Pleasant slabs, first yellow, then white, past several pegs to the foot of a compact grey slab.

2.   25m 5b/c. Climb the slab and a short vertical wall.

3.   30m 4c/5a. A vertical corner leads to a slab, followed by a crack on the right.

4.   25m 5b. Climb the small corner to an overhanging exit. Follow a small ledge rightwards, then a solid white slab to a good

ledge.

5.   25m 5c/6a A0 (6b free). An awkward overhanging arête left of the stance (5b/c) leads to a traverse left along the lip of an overhang to reach an impending arête with 3 bolts. Climbed free, clipping the second of these is probably the crux. Otherwise use 1 or 2 points of aid (with some difficulty!).

6.   25m 5b. Direct up the overhanging wall above, then trend right to climb a small reddish wall.

7.   40m 4b. Follow cracks and grooves over slightly suspect rock, passing several pegs to the top.

Right of Supernova is:

2.   **Tempi Duri**   200m 5c/A0 (6b free)
Battistella & Di Bono

1.   35m 5a. Follow a slab direct to reach a slanting ramp on the left. Continue by way of a thin crack, traversing left from the end of this to the foot of a corner. Up this for 15m to the first stance.

2.   30m 5a. Follow the corner above the belay to a ledge. Up a slab, with a short rightward traverse to another ledge, and climb an overhanging wall to the next belay.

3.   30m 4b/c. A slab leads to a small crack. Traverse left for 5m, then directly up the slab to a small, smooth corner. Follow this to a stance on a block below a grey compact slab.

4.   25m 5b. Climb the superb, nodule covered slab, first direct, then traversing 6m to the foot of a corner. Up this to a stance.

5.   40m 5c/A1 (or a short section of 6b free). Traverse left to an overhanging crack, and climb this to a ledge. Layback the vertical crack past an overhang to a roof. Climb this direct to belay just above.

6.   40m 4b/c. An open corner leads to the end of the difficulties.

Further right are three more recommended climbs:

3.   **Siddharta**   170m 5c. (S.Trentarossi)

4.   **Sincronicita**   150m 5b. (B.Manicardi)

5.   **Paralisi**   40m 5c. (Battistella & Battisti)
(A direct on Sincronicita.)

MONTE PROCINTO

The only other English climber I know to have visited Procinto, described it as a 'little paradise in the mountains', and to a rock climber who is prepared to walk for 45 minutes to get away from the madding crowds it is very close to that. Although from a distance it resembles a Dolomitic tower, on closer acquaintance the rock is a beautifully solid limestone, liberally punctuated with huge solution pockets. No one finger *gouttes* here, most will take at least one hand, many two and some will easily take your head ... As the main east face is rarely less than vertical, the resulting routes are very much in the classic bucket hauling mould - save your fingers for the short nasties on the Zona delle Cattiverie.

   Procinto is the most southerly crag in this present volume, and being only ten miles inland from the acres of burning sands and roasting bodies of Italy's Blackpool (culminating in Viareggio) it is perhaps surprising to find that the climbing season lasts only from June to September. However, with the base of the crag at 1,000 metres in the foothills of the Alpi Apuane and almost all the worthwhile climbing lying on the east and north faces, climbing is virtually impossible outside this period and the best months are actually July and August. Procinto is thus invaluable for those who find Finale, Muzzerone or Bismantova too hot in August (although the combination of these four crags would make a useful mini-tour), or for anyone wishing to combine a few days climbing with either culture vulturing in the nearby cities of Pisa, Lucca or Florence, or a holiday in the hills of Tuscany. The famous marble quarries of Carrera are not far off the autostrada, and the whole area is riddled with small quarries. With little climbing below HVS, the best of the long climbs are in the E1/2 grade, with a good number of shorter routes in the 6a-6c range. On the longer routes protection is almost entirely by pegs and in-situ threads, plus a few bolts, whereas the shorter climbs are mostly spit protected.

Access and Accommodation
Travelling south on the main Genoa-Florence autostrada (the A12

Autostrada del Sole) take the turning for Versilia 25 miles after the La Spezia turning. After 2 miles turn right for Querceta, and after another mile turn left for Seravezza/Castelnuova G. Continue through Seravezza towards Stazzema, leaving this road by forking right at a small blue Carabinieri sign - the crags are just visible above the trees to the right. Follow this small road for just under a mile, then turn right up an obvious track - about 14 miles from the autostrada. Either (1) park at the beginning of the track and follow the path uphill, continuing uphill at an obvious fork to pass a fountain and eventually to the rifugio. Or (2) continue along the track for just over half a mile until it ends at a large parking place. Follow the obvious path uphill - at first steeply through rocks with a steel cable - to reach the fountain and thus the rifugio. The latter is the usual approach, but either. Both are pleasant walks through shady chestnuts, and are never uncomfortably steep. Just before the rifugio, the main tower of Monte Procinto and its smaller satellites La Bimba, Piccolo Procinto and Torrione Bacci are clearly visible on the left. Continue rightwards to reach the Rifugio Forti Dei Marmi (dell Alpe della Grotta) 865m - allow 45 minutes to one hour.

The rifugio is well run with a friendly *ambiente*, and is certainly recommended. The evening meals are usually eaten on a pleasant terrace overlooking the crag, the food and local wines are both very good and prices are low - and with blankets available it is not even necessary to carry a sleeping bag up. Weekends are the busiest times, and even then the hut occupants are likely to be mainly trekkers; on weekdays the hut is generally *tranquillo*. Good water is available from the spring outside the hut, and ice-creams inside.

Guidebooks
Although it is now hopelessly out of date, the old CAI guidebook to the Alpi Apuane contains many of the classics, plus an interesting section on both the geology and the many extensive cave networks of the area (said to include some of the deepest in Europe). This is usually available for reference in the hut, as is the much more useful new routes book which contains a complete set of topos to almost all the climbs.

Approach
From the hut walk back a short distance along the access path to where another path cuts sharply back uphill. Zig-zag up this for five minutes before walking horizontally right for 70/80 metres

121

beneath a subsidiary cliff. Scramble up a gully/stream bed, then return horizontally leftwards underneath the huge 200 metre plus impending face of Il Nona (artificial routes only - rotten rock). Continue to cross a footbridge over a small gorge to arrive at the foot of the Zona delle Cattiverie at the beginning of the east face.

Zona delle Cattiverie

The Zona delle Cattiverie is the smooth black wall overlooking the footbridge. It is defined on the left by a huge roof at about one third height, and on the right by an obvious broken white pillar. With its smooth rock and smaller, more widely spaced pockets, the climbing here is the most technical to be found at Procinto. At the time of our visit there were already 12 routes and variants crammed into this small area - and no doubt by the time this guide-book appears there will be more to add to the confusion! The routes are enjoyably short - one or two pitches to fixed abseil points - and range from 5b/c to 6c, with the majority 6b and above. The main lines are given below, but as they are all well protected by bolts and pegs perhaps the best approach is to select a likely line and give it a try. More details can be found in the new routes book at the rifugio. The climbs are listed from left to right.

Near the right-hand end of the roof is a smooth hanging slab with a small cave-like depression at its foot. This is the line of **Sciocca Bambina**   6b.   Viglani & Pacini

La Tigre Elettrica   (6b/c) starts just right and makes short horizontal traverse to cross Sciocca Bambini a few metres up before following a line to the left.

Il Volo dell'Aquilone   E2 5b/c
Follow a line of weakness steeply left, passing several holes, to a niche. Pass a small but obvious nose on the left with difficulty and move up and right to a chain belay directly above the start.

From here there are three alternatives: (1) abseil off, (2) continue by another pitch of 5c, or (3) follow a horizontal traverse line leftwards above the lip of the great roof (6a).

Starting a few metres up Il Volo is a line of black bolts trending right: **Nervo Calm**   6b/c.

The line of red bolts to the right is **Aglio .... Ragazzo Mio**   E3 6a.

Right again is: **Spit Spit Bang Bang**   6b.   Viglani & Pacini.

Further right, but just left of the main pillar is a small subsidiary

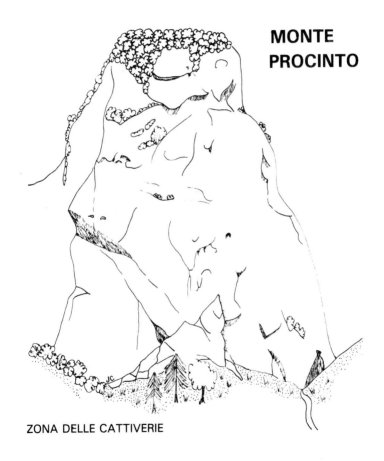

MONTE
PROCINTO

ZONA DELLE CATTIVERIE

pillar. Starting from the top of this is: **Buffulo Bucolico**   6a.

Right again: **Machinegun Kelly**   6c.   Viglani & Pacini.

The East Face

The white pillar marks the beginning of the main 150 metre east face, which has several large caves at its foot. As the rock tends to deteriorate towards the summit, most routes finish at abseil chains on the ledge system at about two thirds height. Starting from the top of the pillar is Gabriela - a fairly direct line in 4 pitches of 6a, 5c, 5c, 5b. Just right of the pillar is:

La Vie en Rose   25m E2 5c

Start below a small roof with a large thread in its left-hand side. Abseil off or follow two more pitches of 5b/c, 5b, and abseil from a fixed point to the right of the third stance.

To the right, several routes have a common easy first pitch, including the two subsequent pitches of the direct and very sustained **La Danza Dei Tendini** (5c), which has an alternative second pitch - **Presagio** (6c?).

Right again, and reached by scrambling up broken rocks diagonally leftwards from the point where the path almost meets the foot of the face is:

Tropicana   135m HVS/E1 5b

G.Malera 1964

1.   An easy, almost horizontal rightward traverse leads to a belay above the left-hand end of the first cave.

2.   Three alternative pitches can be taken to the next stance, direct is 5a (the normal route), to the left or right 5b.

3.   5a. Continue more or less direct.

4.   5b. Diagonally left, then fairly direct before returning right to reach the ledge. Walk slightly rightward along this to belay/abseil chains.

Descent

With 50m ropes two abseils lead directly to the ground. (1) 50m to chains (possible to split at several points. (2) 45m over the cave to the ground.

From the second stance of Tropicana, and keeping to the right of that route, is the more direct and slightly harder line of **Super Craig** (spits).

The first cave has an overhanging pillar on its right side with two large threads about 4 metres above the ground.

Confessione di una Strega. (A Witch's Confessions)   100m E2 5b
One of the best of the middle grade classics here - enjoyable, strenuous climbing on good rock with excellent protection - mainly by threads. Some of these are rather old so carry a few tapes for re-threading. Pitches 1 and 4 are very sustained.

1.   35m 5b. Climb the pillar (crux) exiting left onto a ledge, then up fairly directly to a large thread at 25/30m. Move diagonally right to a stance.

2.   25m 5a. Traverse horizontally left for 6m, move up the pillar for a few metres then go diagonally right to a stance (care needed with the rock in a few obvious places).

3.   20m 5a. Move left for 2m, up fairly directly for 10m, then more easily diagonally leftwards over broken rock to a stance in a shallow cave.

4.   20m 5b. Leave the cave on the right and move up to a series of flakes leading slightly rightwards to a thread. Climb directly up to a ledge and traverse several metres left along this to belay and abseil as for Tropicana.

Towards the right of the east face is the largest of the caves, which has a large bridge-like pillar running across its roof. This is the: Settore dell Circo. A number of very strenuous routes climb the roof. From left to right these are:

Space Shuttle   6b/c.

Lama di Rasolo   6a.

Peggio Che Andar di Notte Senza Fari   6c.

Conolente   6c.

The North Face

The path continues to the right beneath the north face. Less steep and continuous, the rock here is broken by corners and bulges.

The arête separating the east and north faces is taken by:
Oli Volá   25m E1 5b
Strenuous climbing with superb holds and protection leads first direct, then left, before returning right to a stance beneath a hanging arête. Abseil off or continue by another short pitch of 6a - the direct variant to the first stance is said to be 6b.

The next climb starts just to the right by scrambling up some 8 or 10 metres below a small pillar to a thread belay.

Dolfi-Melucci 100m HVS 5a
 Dolfi & Melucci 1955

Despite a somewhat dirty first pitch and a little loose rock on pitch
3, this remains an enjoyable and worthwhile expedition - particularly as it is the only climb described here to reach the summit.
Carry thin tape or rope slings for threading.

1. 30m 4b. A rising traverse leads rightwards around bulges to a
stance and thread belays below an overlap.

2. 25m 5a. Up slightly right, then follow the line of the overlap to
its apex. Bridge up to, then climb directly over the roof (strenuous)
to a stance with pegs and thread belays 4 metres above.

3. 50m 5a (for a very short section). Climb straight up behind
the belay to a bulge at 8 metres (bolt). Move left onto a ramp (poor
rock) and climb the corner above (obvious from the path below),
before stepping right into a niche on the arête (possible poor
stance - pegs). Climb the slab on the right to another niche, then
move right onto a smooth undercut slab. Climb this (crux) moving
up and leftwards to belay on bolts.

Descent

Scramble up and rightwards around an arête into a mossy gully.
Follow a faint path up to and over the summit, and descend to the
top of the via ferrata. Descend this, taking care not to dislodge
rocks, and follow the path back around to the right (facing in) to
return to the east face.

BISMANTOVA

Over 100m in height and more than a quarter of a mile in width, the great fortress of Bismantova bears a close resemblance to one of the buttes or mesas of Arizona so familiar from the films of John Ford. Its surroundings are equally unusual - rolling hills patterned by a mosaic of fields and woodland reminiscent of Germany's Rheinpfalz.

The rock is a strange limey sandstone, solid in the newly developed areas of bolt-protected climbs near the foot of the cliff, more friable in other parts. Although there are routes on the SE and SW faces, the best of the climbing is to be found on the main south face. The great crack/chimney lines were naturally the scene of the earliest explorations, and although a large number of these still involve aid (usually from in-situ peg-bolts) they have become the classics of today. The earliest of these is the **Via Degli Svizzeri** (1922) which now gives a long expedition at Very Difficult standard. In 1986 the first climbing competition for 'amateurs' was held here, and the excellent short routes on the Zona delle Gare mostly date from this time, with another area of short, enjoyable climbs on the extreme right of the main face.

The summit plateau is a huge grassy meadow with extensive views in all directions, easily reached by either of two waymarked paths to the left (west) of the main face, which also form the descent routes. The red is the longer and easier (15 minutes), the blue (10 minutes) forks off to the right shortly after the start, and involves a short section of moderate scrambling amongst interesting rock-architecture. There is also a via ferrata on the eastern side. A summit bivouac is highly recommended, particularly in spring when the meadow is carpeted with wild flowers. In the Verdon-style there are now several groups of one pitch climbs reached by abseil from the summit; as most of these are very difficult to find and sometimes take poor rock, only a small number of easily located and worthwhile ones have been included.

Although not recommended as a major objective for a holiday, Bismantova is certainly worth a visit - especially when combined

128   *Bismantova - Al Churcher on Blade Runner, E4 6b*
        Photo: Jill Churcher

with a trip to Muzzerone or Procinto. Climbing is possible here during most of the year, although it is at its best in spring and autumn. However, by climbing in the mornings and late afternoon/ early evenings we had three enjoyable days here in mid-August.

Access, Camping etc.
To Reggio Emilia via the A1 autostrada from Milan via Piacenza and Parma, then an easy 30 miles to the small holiday town of Castelnovo ne'Monti. From here follow signs for 'La Pietra di Bismantova' (NOT those which simply say 'Bismantova') - about 2 miles.

From La Spezia it is a slow, but very scenic drive of some 2 hours (60 miles) via the Passo dell Ceretto (1,261m - good view over the Alpi Apuane to the SW).

There is a campsite in Castelnovo (signposted from the town) and a rifugio immediately below the crag. The rifugio also contains the new routes book, guidebooks, and is an invaluable source of ice-creams on hot days (not to mention spinach flans and torta ....).

Guidebooks
La Pietra di Bismantova - Aimi & Righetti. Pub. Melograno '86.

A strong candidate for the worst guidebook of all time award. With no access notes it is the perfect example of a guidebook written for people who already know the routes. Apart from those reached by abseil, the newer short free climbs are not included. Only worth purchasing by those intending to climb more of the long routes than are described here.

Approach
From the car park follow steps and a wide path to a small piazza and church - the rifugio is on the left just before the church. For obvious reasons climbing is completely banned on the grey pillar above the church. A wide paved path leads leftwards, soon narrowing to a dirt path - the beginning of the waymarked paths to the summit. Some fifty yards along, the path passes directly beneath the Zona delle Gare, an area of one-pitch spit-protected climbs bounded on the left by a 20m high broken pillar, and to the right by a low dry-stone wall. Some fifty metres further along the path is a small detached tower - the Campanile CTG - the chimney behind this giving the first pitch of **Via Elisa** (VS/A1). The wall to the right of the campanile has two newish bolted routes:

129

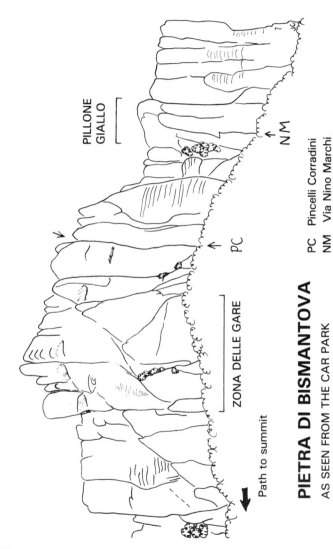

PILLONE GIALLO

NM

PC

ZONA DELLE GARE

Path to summit

PIETRA DI BISMANTOVA

AS SEEN FROM THE CAR PARK

PC   Pincelli Corradini
NM   Via Nino Marchi

Porta sul Futura   25m 6b/c (the left-hand route).
Illusioni   25m 6a (to the right).

ZONA DELLE GARE

The obvious jam-crack in the pillar defining this area on the left is the start of the **Via Zuffa Ruggiero** which makes a good, well protected 5b pitch in its own right, the other 4 pitches being of a much easier standard.

Just right of this pillar is a blackish impending wall, severely undercut at its base. In shadow until 11.00a.m. in mid-August, this is taken by four difficult but well protected routes, all finishing at fixed abseil chains. The name of the left-hand route is unknown, but it is obviously at least 6b, whereas the central line taking the small roof at 4 metres is: **Bla Bla Bla**   15m 6c   (Mariacher (?) '86).

The undercut arête to the right again is: **Blade Runner**   15m E4 6b.

Just right of the arête is another superb climb taking a direct line up the steep wall;
Il Muro Sconosciuto   15m E3 6a
On the right, past another small pillar, is a bolted slabby wall with three enjoyable 20m routes in the HVS/E1 5b range. A second wall further to the right has another 3 routes of 5b/c - all rather steeper but with closer bolts.

THE SOUTH FACE

Just right of the dry-stone wall is an easy angled protruding buttress with a crack up the centre - the start of:
Via degli Svizzeri   135m Very Difficult
   Voltolini 1922
Follow the obvious line of cracks and corners in 6 pitches, finishing up a slab bearing rightwards. The hardest pitches at the first and last.

The path continues rightwards to end at an obvious wide chimney starting at a cave some 2 or 3 metres up. This is:
Pincelli Corradini   130m E1 5b (HVS 5a with 2 points of aid)
   Pincelli and Corradini 1940
Although starting just left of the edge of the piazza, the start

cannot be reached from there. A fine steep and varied classic following a natural line up a series of corners, it has something of the atmosphere of a Gogarth route, marred only by a short dirty section at the beginning of pitch 2 and the slightly worrying nature of the rock at the crux (although this is well protected). Generally good protection but with very spaced bolts on pitch 2. Carry rocks 7-9 or medium hexes/Friends. As the upper pitches are above the piazza *climbing is banned at weekends.*

Start by scrambling up to the shady cave.

1.   25m 4b.Climb the right-hand chimney to a ledge below an overhanging pillar (1 bolt at half-height).

2.   45m 4c. Move easily right and climb the obvious corner, at first easy and rather dirty, soon becoming steep enjoyable climbing on good rock and with large holds - often with the aid of a crack on the right wall. Belay at a ledge beneath a tree at the top of the corner.

3.   40m 5b. Climb a steep little wall above the stance then move diagonally right around a small tree to regain the line of the corner. (Possible belay - 3 bolts - not recommended as this is in a direct line of any stonefall from the roof above.) The direct variant is on appalling rock and is similarly not recommended. Continue up the corner passing a small overhang with difficulty (crux - slightly worrying rock. The use of the bolt on the right wall and a Friend 2 for aid would reduce this to a strenuous 5a). Exit above and move diagonally right to a tree and bolt belay (the dead branches of this tree are visible from the second stance).

4.   20m 4c. Climb the chimney above to a ledge on the right (thread). Continue up the wall above, using a large crack on the right and a flake/groove on the left. An exposed and exhilarating pitch.

Returning to the piazza, the first area to the right is the aptly named and easily recognizable L'Anfiteatro. The most popular area at Bismantova it contains a number of routes and variation, mostly in the VS/HVS grades. Many of these are equipped with chains for abseil descents.

Right of the amphitheatre is the obvious yellow pillar of the:

Pillone Giallo

The obvious corner on the left of the pillar is taken by one of the best of the longer climbs. The crux pitch is strenuous, and although there is a fair amount of in-situ protection a set of

Davide Battistella on Diario nel Sole E4/6b, Bismantova
                    Photo: Al Churcher

medium/large hexes or Friends should be carried.

Via Nini Marchi   E2 5b

Vigo & Pandolfo 1971

Start at an obvious large flake to the left of the crack line.

1.   30m. Easily up the flake to a peg, traverse horizontally right then diagonally rightwards, firstly by a thin crack then by means of a slab to a ledge.

2.   25m 5a. Good climbing up the corner above to reach a large terrace.

3.   45m 5b. Continue up the overhanging corner passing a small roof at about thirty metres to a restricted stance.

4.   35m 4c. Diagonally leftwards to a flake, surmount this and follow the easy corner to the summit.

To the right of the foot of the Pillone Giallo are a number of large boulders. Behind these is a very large flake about 5m above the ground. The corner crack is the first pitch of Zuffa Modini, said to be worthwhile (30m 5a, abseil off or continue by two pitches of A2 and one of A3). Right of this is the second area of recent bolted climbs, identified by the words 'Pronto Soccorso' painted on the rock (the apt name for the loose crack above - it means First Aid...). The impending arête immediately right is: **Diario nel Sole**   20m E4 6b.

Right again, and arriving at the same abseil chains is the shallow corner crack of: **Nannunzi Brandi**   20m HVS 5a.

Good climbing and protection makes this an excellent introductory route. Right of this is a short overhanging jam-crack to a tree - **Vedo Nero** - 10m 6a - and the obvious jam-crack is the first pitch of **Via Cai Parma**   27m 5b/c - well protected by bolts on the left wall - abseil off as the upper pitches are A1, 2 & 3.

The Summit Climbs

As mentioned earlier, only a small number of these are described here. The following are worthwhile, particularly for a short route or two to finish off the day after the completion of one of the long routes to the summit. All are on good rock, and although protected by bolts would be easy to top-rope. At the highest point of the summit plateau on its eastern edge, are the remains of a wooden flagpole. Directly below this are two bolts forming the abseil point for:

Welcome to Badolo   30m 6b/c

Steep and technical, with a monster reach at one point.

   10m right (looking out) is another pair of bolts. Abseil from these to 2 belay bolts right of the obvious arête.

   More or less direct, keeping right of the arête is:

Alba Chiara   35m HVS/E1 5a/b

Steep, enjoyable climbing on big holds, on excellent rock.

Bonnye   35m HVS/E1 5a/b

Similar climbing, moving right from the same stance.

For those of an adventurous nature, there are several other routes in this area said to be worth finding; an excellent VS/HVS corner gained by an abseil from pegs just to the left (facing out) of the wooden flagstaff is **Oklahoma Sooners**   35m 4c, breaking out left a few metres from the stance of this is **Boh**   35m 5c. Thirty metres left of the flagstaff is a tree near the edge, an abseil from this gains (hopefully) the foot of **Il Gatto Che Si Morde La Coda**   35m 5c. Left again is the grassy gully of the last pitch of **Spigolo dei Nasi** and **Via del Diedro**. Left again is the abseil bolt for **Oggi le Comiche** and **Per Un Soffio di Magnesite** (both 15m 6a).

ARCO

Arco - or more correctly the Valle di Sarca - was one of the forcing grounds of the first wave of free climbing to hit Italy in the early 80's, and the presence of the names Mariacher, Bassi and Zanolla (better known as 'Manolo') on so many first ascents bears ample witness to this.

As befits its position, many routes are Dolomitic in both length and character, e.g. those on Cima Colodri. However, the area is perhaps better known for its short bolt-protected routes on 'roadside crags' such as Spiaggia della Lucertole with its clutch of hard climbs on perfect pocketed limestone. Add the long slab climbs of the Placche Zebrate - including a number of excellent routes in the lower grades - and Arco has much to offer climbers of most standards. The favourable climate allows climbing virtually throughout the year, and the windsurfing (Garda is renowned for its winds, and Torbole is the home of the Italian sailboard team), and other attractions of Lake Garda, plus the proximity of the Dolomites make it an excellent centre for crag-rats, refugees from storm-lashed mountains, and family holidays.

Approach
Arco lies just SW of Trento at the head of Lake Garda. It is easily reached from the autostrada running south from the Brenner Pass via Bolzano, which meets the Milan-Venice autostrada at the southern end of the lake. The direct approach from Mello is by a slow, but spectacular journey via the passes of Aprica and Tonale.

Guidebooks, Camping etc.
The guidebook *Arrampicare in Valle di Sarca* by Roberto Bassi, pub. Zanichelli '84, can be found at Tomasoni, Via Maffei 8, Piazza del Erbe, Riva del Garda. Riva is an interesting medieval town, and less expensive than its thronging tourists would suggest. Its fruit and vegetable market is particularly recommended.

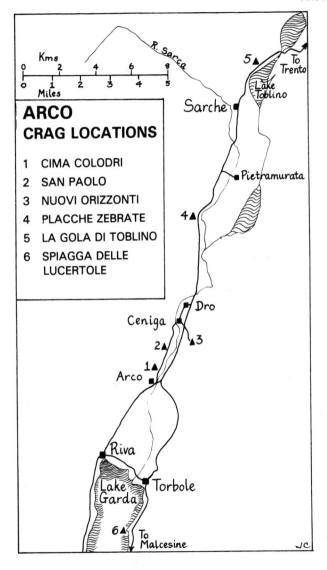

Kms

ARCO
CRAG LOCATIONS

1 CIMA COLODRI
2 SAN PAOLO
3 NUOVI ORIZZONTI
4 PLACCHE ZEBRATE
5 LA GOLA DI TOBLINO
6 SPIAGGA DELLE
   LUCERTOLE

A number of large expensive campsites are to be found near the lake, but most climbers stay on the much cheaper site near the village of Arco itself. Going north from Arco, a minor road to Ceniga and Dro runs parallel to the main Trento road. The campsite lies just outside Arco on this road. (Bivouacs possible in the olive trees behind.) This site is particularly convenient for climbs on Colodri. For short stays, pleasant bivouacs can be found on the beaches along the eastern shore of the lake.

CIMA COLODRI - (S.E. Face)

The large cliff almost directly behind the campsite to the north of Arco has a number of Dolomite-style routes. On excellent rock, the climbing is both interesting and varied, with exciting situations. All the climbs are free, although there are many pegs in place. By taking advantage of the morning sun in winter, and the afternoon shade in summer, climbing is possible throughout the year.

It is usual to gear up at the campsite, from which the climbs can be reached in a few minutes. Descent is by a via ferrata on the south side of the crag, i.e. to the right looking out.

The climbs are described from right to left.

Barbara   310m E1 5b/c
   Ischia & Ischia 11/72
The classic of the cliff, taking the obvious corner to the right of the large pillar high up on the right-hand side of the face. Start at the foot of an obvious slabby break leading diagonally rightwards.
1.   35m 4c. Climb a slab beneath a yellow wall, then make a long easy rightward traverse to the foot of a small slanting chimney.
2.   40m 5a. Climb this and the flake crack above.
3.   40m 4c. Follow the ramp rightwards to a stance on a small pillar.
4.   40m 5b/c. Traverse the horizontal crack rightwards, then climb more or less directly up a slab and crack to the foot of the great corner.
5.   40m 5a. Good, strenuous climbing up the polished corner.
6.   20m. Traverse easily rightwards by a friable ledge.
7.   40m 4c. Climb a crack to enter a chimney. Follow this to belay on the second jammed block.
8.   30m 5b. Climb the crack on the left strenuously to a ledge.
9.   25m 4a. Easily left, then up a short wall.

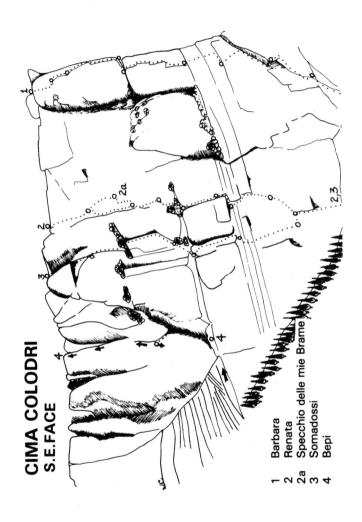

CIMA COLODRI
S.E.FACE

1   Barbara
2   Renata
2a   Specchio delle mie Brame
3   Somadossi
4   Bepi

Via Renata   295m E2 5c
  Furlani et al 2/79

A sustained route following a series of flakes and corners on excellent rock. Particularly recommended with the variation pitches of Specchio, which take the standard up to E3 6a.

Approach

Walk along the road from the swimming pool to a small car park, and go up scree to the foot of the face.

1.   40m 4c. Climb a grey corner to a large ledge (Somadossi continues left from here.)

2.   25m 4c. Follow the ledge right, overcome a roof and go up to the top of a small pilar. (**Katia** continues rightwards.)

3.   25m 5a. A flake crack with good holds leads to the foot of a long roof.

4.   25m 5b. Make an exposed rightward traverse beneath the roof, and go up to a stance.

5.   45m 5c. Climb the corner to a ledge and trees.

6.   35m 5b. A corner on the right leads to another ledge and trees.

7.   30m 4c. A reddish corner leads to a ledge on the right.

8.   30m 4c. Up to a black overhang and climb it by means of a crack. Move round an arête and up to a stance.

9.   40m 5a. Direct up cracked slabs to the top.

Variante Specchio delle mie Brame
(The Mirror of my Desires)   60m E3 6a
  Bassi & Mariacher 3/82

An excellent variant from the sixth stance above.

7.   30m 5b. Follow the reddish corner for 3 or 4m, traverse right around the arête to a peg, then return left. Go up, first direct, then rightwards to a stance.

8.   30m 6a. Excellent climbing up the cracked slab above, to rejoin the parent route at the 8th stance.

Somadossi   300m E2 5c
  Bassi & Giacomelli '79

1.   40m 4c. As for Renata to the first stance.

2.   20m. Walk left to the foot of an obvious detached pillar (possible belay).

3.   40m 5b. Climb the pillar to its top (possible belay). Move rightwards across a steep wall below a roof to a ledge.

4.   50m 5c. Easily rightwards to the foot of a large corner (possible belay). Climb the crack in the left face of the corner, then

140

small cracks in the white slab above. Finally traversing left to a ledge with trees.

5. 25m 4c. Follow the chimney-crack diagonally rightwards to trees.

6. 45m 4c. Continue up the corner to a ledge and more trees.

7/8. 55m 4c/5a. Two pitches up steep cracks and corners to a roof easily visible from below.

9. 25m 4c. Traverse rightwards to enter another corner and follow this to the summit.

South Face - Bepi   30m E3 6a
  Leviti & Salvaterra 6/80

A good wall climb taking the left edge of the obvious cave in the south face. Start by ascending the via ferrata and traversing right to the foot of the cave.

1. 30m 6a. Climb the crack up to the overhang. Over this and follow slabs to a stance. Well protected.

  Either abseil off or continue by a series of chimneys and corners up to 5a for another 140m (4 pitches).

SAN PAOLO

The three faces known collectively as San Paolo lie below and right (north) of Colodri. From the campsite go about one third of a mile north along the minor road towards the hamlet of Ceniga. The first cliff (Promontorio di Kroz) can be clearly seen on the left, about 100m from the road. Walk up through trees. Routes are spit-protected, although a few nuts and Friends can be useful. The climbing is steep and fingery, often utilizing tiny flakes or 'ears', for holds.

The Promontorio di Kroz

Distinguished by a large ledge running diagonally upwards from left to right. The main pitches all start from this, although there are a number of pitches up the wall below the ledge (all 6a/b). The routes were all climbed in 1982 by A.Leviti, with either A.Giambisi or R.Bassi.

  Descent is by a path through the trees towards Colodri.

  The two routes starting from the left of the ledge share a common start to just below the obvious roof. **Pioneer**   35m E4 6a, takes the roof on its left, then the crack above.

Super Tilt   35m E4 6a, takes the roof on its right, then a crack.

Further right is **Obelix**   35m E2 5c. The initial roof is 5c when climbed on the left, 5b on the right.

The Pilastro delle Vergini

The next area to the right is reached by a short path leading north from the foot of Kroz, as there is no direct approach from the road. The climbs were the product of Bassi and Monolo in 1983, and descents are by abseil.

Bip-bip   60m E4 6a/b, is the left-hand route, starting from an obvious niche.

Gri-grill   55m E5 6a/b, lies to the right.

Basta con la Cioccolata   50m E1/2 5b/c takes the right-hand corner.

Muro delle Civette

Return to the road and continue along this for another 250m before taking a path up through the trees.

Starting up a rightward slanting corner from a ledge on the extreme left of the face is:
Swing   30m E5 6b (Mariacher & Guerrini 5/83). Abseil off.

An extended version is:
Super Swing   50m E6 6b/c
Mariacher & Bassi 5/83
By continuing direct where Swing moves left to belay, this makes a very sustained pitch. Splitting it makes it easier, but the locals won't count it as a genuine ascent!

On the extreme right is **Sirac en'rut**   30m E3 5c/6a. Abseil off.

NUOVI ORIZZONTI

Facing SW, the climbing on Nuovi Orizzohti is similar in character to that of the smaller Spiaggia della Lucertole. On good rock, the climbs are well bolted, and some stances equipped for abseil.

Approach
About 2 miles north of Arco on the main Trento road (SS45b) is a

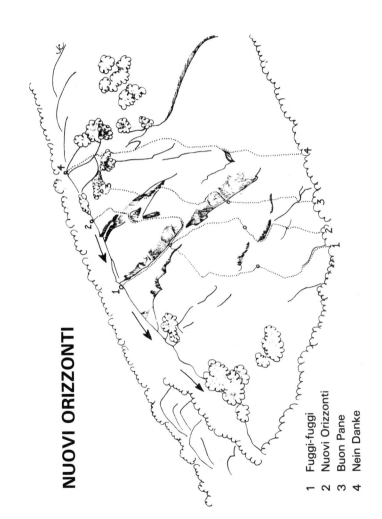

NUOVI ORIZZONTI

1 Fuggi-fuggi
2 Nuovi Orizzonti
3 Buon Pane
4 Nein Danke

turning left for Ceniga and Dro. Opposite this, a track leads up through trees to the foot of the crag (which is visible from the road). An interesting 5-10 minute walk.

Descent
From the top of the routes, go back a few metres through trees from the cliff edge, and follow a path leading down left to return to the foot of the crag.

The climbs are described from left to right.

Fuggi-fuggi   75m E2 5c. (Mariacher & Jovane) Spring '83.

Nuovi Orizzonti   75m E3 5c
   Leviti & Bernard 10/82
Starting at the same point then taking a line to the right, is the original route of the crag. This rejoins Fugi-fugi at the second stance, moves rightwards under a roof to gain a corner, and finishes to the right of this.

A variation first pitch to the right is **Recia del Diaol**   6a.

Buon Pane   60m E4 6a
   Mariacher, Zanolla & Bassi 5/83
A fairly direct line to an abseil point some 15m below the highest point of the cliff, via an obvious roof above the first stance.

Some way right is **Mago Volante**   6b which also finishes below the top, and just right again is the easiest route on the cliff.

Nein Danke   75m E1 5b
   Vettori et al
Follow a line of corners and cracks past two roofs to the top. Medium nuts and some Friends useful.

LE PLACCHE ZEBRATE

With its good selection of long easy routes, as well as a number of harder ones, it is understandable that this should be one of the most popular crags in the area. Said by some to be reminiscent of the 'Apron', the relaxing slab climbing is in pleasant contrast to the steep, fingery climbing of the other crags described here. The names of the climbs are written below, and the line of most routes is indicated with paint. Carry a good selection of nuts, and thin slings for threads.

Approach
About half-way along the road from Dro to Pietramura is a large fish-farm. Park here and follow a track leading towards the obvious slabs above (west). A path then breaks off to the screes at the foot of the slabs. 15 minutes.

Descent
From the summit, a path leads down screes, 15 minutes.

Claudia   600m VS 4c
Bertoldi, Colpo & Zeni 3/78

The first route to be encountered above the scree. Though the climbing is not continuous, the individual pitches are good. The route marked includes the Rossi Variant, which has become the accepted way.

Rita   550m V.Diff
Rossi & Andreotti 3/71

The easiest route on the slabs, taking first a friable slab, and then following a chimney.

Gabri-Camilla   350m E3 5b
Giovannetti & Cagol '80

One of the best climbs here, but with a bold fourth pitch (15 metre run out).

Amicizia   400m E3 5c
Furlani & Weiss 12/78

The second and third pitches take a fine compact slab protected by peg-bolts - the line of which can be seen from below. The other pitches are much easier.

Abbracadavere   50m E3 5c/6a
Bassi 9/82

Near the bottom of the descent path is a triangular shaped compact slab. Abbracadavere takes the centre of this by a line of bolts. N.B. From the fourth spit traverse left for 4/5 metres to a stance.

There are now a number of other short bolt-protected routes in the area.

LA GOLA DI TOBLINO (The Toblino Gorge)

Just outside the Valle di Sarca, about 10 miles north of Arco and 8 west of Trento, is the small lake of Toblino. Between the head of the lake and the main SS45b Arco-Trento road is a lakeside castle (now the 'Ristorante Castel Toblino'). A small road leads off opposite this to the gorge. Park outside the entrance, from where a short walk leads to the various buttresses. With one exception, all 6 of these are on the right side of the gorge as you enter it.

Development started in late 1984, mostly by Roberto Bassi, with a number of notable contributions by Maurizio Zanolla (Manolo). Although the buttress of Il Castello is said to offer delicate slab climbs, most of the climbs are the steep fingery extremes to be expected on modern spit-protected limestone, and in the list of 31 routes first published by *Alp* in July 1986, only 5 were less than 6a, with a number of 6c. Most of the climbs are of 1 pitch, although a few have a second. Names are painted below.

The gorge is at its best in autumn, when the river is dry and temperatures reasonable; spring is also good, but with the river full and noisy, humidity is also high. Like Arco the summer is very hot, although the gorge is too shaded for winter climbing.

Toblino The Climbs

	Pitch 1.	2.	
Don Camillo	6a		M.Zanolla
Tursen	6c		M.Zanolla
007	6c-		H.Mariacher
Impedita	6c		M.Zanolla
Roulette Russa	6a −		R.Bassi
Ercolino	6a		R.Bassi
Morbillio	5c		F.Rivis
Rapsodie	5a	6b +	R.Bassi
Tendinete	6a	6a	R.Bassi
Dollarie & Paperi	5b	6b	M.Zanolla
Capitan Cliff	5b +	6c	R.Bassi
Sex Climb	6a		S.Finocchi
Calamici Jane	6b		R.Bassi
Sfinge	6a	7a(?)	M.Zanolla

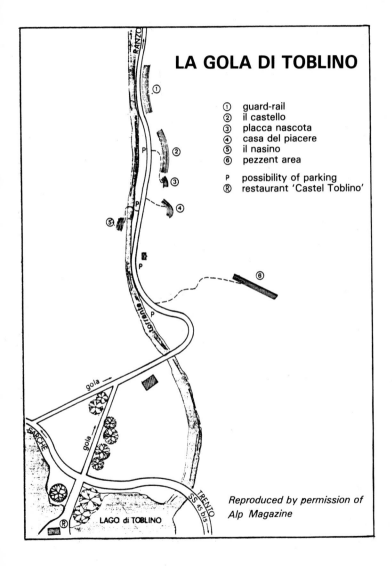

LA GOLA DI TOBLINO

① guard-rail
② il castello
③ placca nascota
④ casa del piacere
⑤ il nasino
⑥ pezzent area

P   possibility of parking
®   restaurant 'Castel Toblino'

*Reproduced by permission of
Alp Magazine*

LAGO di TOBLINO

African Reggae	6b	(?)	R.Bassi
Rasta Way	5c	(?)	L.di Marino
Che Peperino	6a	6a/b	L.di Marino
Bob Rock	6a		R.Bassi
Mister Monkey	6a	6c	Gerard
Cleopatra	6c		R.Bassi
N. Bis	6b		R.Bassi
Band Aids	6a/b		R.Bassi
Madame da Ment	5c		E.Delmut
Le Ore	6b/c		R.Bassi
Minniminopropio	6a		R.Bassi
Spit Terrore	6b		R.Bassi
O in Amore	6a		R.Bassi
Lupperman	5a		A.Fronza
Discopettomane	6a		R.Bassi
Tris di Donne	6c		R.Bassi
Mano di Fatto	6a+		R.Bassi

My thanks to *Alp* magazine and the authors Roberto Bassi, Diego and Leonardo di Marino, for permission to use the list of routes.

SPIAGGIA DELLE LUCERTOLE

Take Verdon's cliff of Miroir du Fou, double it in size and slip it into the edge of Lake Garda and you have 'The Beach of the Lizards' - even down to the road tunnel. Using pockets and small lay-aways on perfect rock, the climbing is both fingery and technical, and the routes superb. Although it faces south, with cooling swims between routes climbing is possible even in August, but inversions and winds often rule-out winter months. Protection is by rather spaced bolts, and a few small to medium nuts can be useful.

Access
From Torbole, near the head of Lake Garda, drive south towards Malcesine passing through 2 galleries. The crag can be clearly seen immediately after the second of these - park here or on the left after the next gallery, (from here a tunnel leads under the road to a small beach - bolt lines on the small crag on the right). Scramble down to water-level and follow via ferrata-type iron spikes just above water-level across the foot of the crag. A useful landmark is the small tree growing out of the rock at the foot of Honky Tonky.

Davide Battistella on Honky Tonky E3 6a -
Spiaggia delle Lucertole, Arco.

Descent

Is by means of a path leading down the left arête of the crag (i.e. that furthest from the road), ending at a small beach with easy slabs above - possibilities for beginners. If you don't mind wet ropes it is easier to abseil, and it is certainly preferable for Luisa Violenta and Tom Tom Club.

The climbs are described from left to right, starting with the easiest and shortest. Following a line of pegs is **Daffy-Daffy** 25m HVS 5a. (Bassi & Martino 11/82).

Three routes are squeezed in between Daffy Daffy and Honky Tonky. The first being **Funky ma Chic** 30m E4 6b. (Bassi 1/83).

Close to this is **Bepi Nero** 30m E4 6b. (Bassi 11/82) and **Piccola Dose** 35m E5 6b/c. (Bassi), a harder right-hand finish to the above.

Honky Tonky 35m E3 6a
Bassi & Degasperi 10/82
The classic of the crag, and one of the most photographed routes in Italy. Start at the small tree just left of the diagonal break.

Cicala Clac E5 6b
Bassi & Zanolla 6/83
An alternative finish to Honky Tonky, continuing more or less direct where that route traverses left beneath the fig tree.

Luisa Violenta 80m E3 6a
Mariacher & Luisa Jovane 9/83
Starting just below the left-hand side of the obvious cave, and climbing the wall to a hanging stance above the diagonal vegetated break, the second pitch begins with a long almost horizontal traverse right. There are two harder finishes.

The first is a more or less direct finish, moving slightly left from the stance. **La Signora degli Appigli** E6 6c. (Zanolla 10/83). The second starts halfway across the traverse **Non Seguitemi, mi sono perso. (Don't Follow Me, I'm Lost)** E5 6b/c. (Mariacher, Zanolla, Bassi '83).

Tom Tom Club 65m E4 5a, 6b
Mariacher & Pederiva 11/83
Starting level with the road, and mid-way between this and the cave, an easy first pitch is followed by a difficult exit.

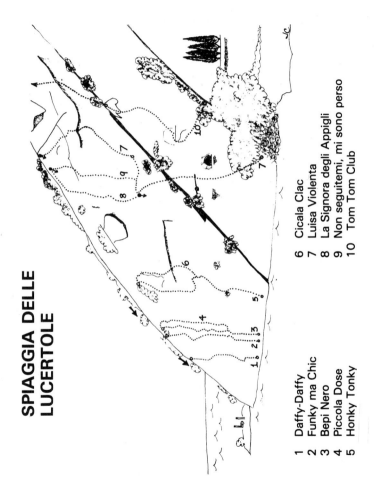

SPIAGGIA DELLE LUCERTOLE

1 Daffy-Daffy
2 Funky ma Chic
3 Bepi Nero
4 Piccola Dose
5 Honky Tonky

6 Cicala Clac
7 Luisa Violenta
8 La Signora degli Appigli
9 Non seguitemi, mi sono perso
10 Tom Tom Club

THE LECCO AREA

The limestone around Lecco has been a popular climbing ground for Italians since the turn of the century. In particular the towers and faces of the Grigne provided a microcosm of the Dolomites for such famous names as Cassin, Panzeri, Corti, Bonatti and Gogna, who left a rich legacy of classic climbs, mainly between 100 and 200 metres long, but up to 600 metres in the Northern Grigna. This is a much neglected area by the British, and with its good network of rifugios, one that would seem to be well-worth exploring. However, the dolomitic nature of the climbing in the Grigna excludes it from the scope of this volume, and the climbs described here are to be found on the easily accessible, solid limestone most suited for modern free climbing, with the addition of some longer routes on Medale.

Although not an area to be chosen as the major objective of a climbing trip, it would combine well with a visit to either Mello or Finale, as well as providing a useful diversion for a family holiday in the Como area. As with the Dolomites, sudden storms can be frequent in high summer, particularly in the Grigne, and some of the crags are very hot at this time of the year. However the NE facing Corno del Nibbio is ideal for hot weather, and with an early start and a breezy day, even the climbs on Medale are possible in August. Spring and autumn are the optimum periods, with climbing possible from March to November.

Access and Camping

The town of Lecco lies at the foot of the right leg of Lake Como (known as the Lago di Lecco), and is easily reached from either Como, or from Milan via Monza, or with more difficulty from the north via Zurich - Chur - Splugen Pass - Chiavenna. As the main industries of the area are agriculture and tourism, rough camping is very hard to find, although it is possible around Piani Resinelli if you are prepared (like Paddington) to look very hard. There are a number of campsites on the lakeside, a caravan/campsite at Piani Resinelli, and another ('Camping Grigna') on the left-hand side of the

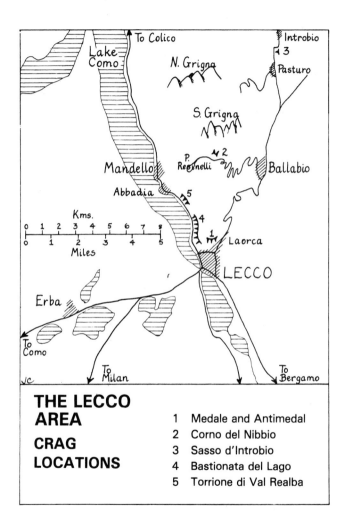

THE LECCO AREA

CRAG LOCATIONS

1. Medale and Antimedal
2. Corno del Nibbio
3. Sasso d'Introbio
4. Bastionata del Lago
5. Torrione di Val Realba

153

Val Sassina road about 2 miles after Ballabio and signposted from there. All are expensive.

Guidebooks
Although older guides exist to the Grigne, the only one covering the areas described below (as well as the Grigne) is:
Arrampicate Scelte nel Lecchese - Casari & Dinoia. Pub. Melograno Edizioni 1985.

A modern topo-style guide which unfortunately contains little access information.

CORNA DI MEDALE

This great bastion of white limestone stands in a commanding position above Lecco. Its long routes have something of the flavour of the Dolomites - but without the scree ledges! On the whole the rock is very good, but the presence of some loose rock means that it is definitely a helmet crag. With its sunny southern aspect, easy access and descent, and long mostly hard climbs, it is probably the most popular of the big cliffs in the area. Although most have been freed, the majority of routes are generally climbed with some aid, and are thus well-equipped with in-situ protection, although a rack of nuts should be carried. Recently a number of fences have been erected to protect the village below from stone-fall, and these have cut right through the old paths which formed the most natural approaches.

Approach
From Lecco follow signs for Val Sassina. At the edge of the built-up area the road makes a hairpin bend to the right. Take a left fork here, which immediately turns back sharply left - green barrier and sign for 'Edlivie S.P.A.'. Follow this road, which soon ends at a wide parking space. Leave the car here and follow an alleyway which rises up to the right. Make a detour below the cemetery then continue zig-zagging up the hillside to the Rifugio Corno Medale - the best place to view the crag as a whole. The path continues uphill until it meets the first of the stone fences. For routes on the right end of Medale, turn right and follow a wide track uphill, past fences leading off to the left to steps through a concrete wall. A small path rejoins the main track - turn left and follow this to the next bend where a small path leads across scree then up through

trees to the subsidiary buttresses to the right of the main cliff.

Known as the Bastionata del Rifugio, this area bears a number of shorter routes which finish either at abseil points, or the terrace level with the fifth pitch of Taveggia. **Calcaria Terminia** (80m HVS) is a worthwhile looking route on clean rock - start marked by a prominent red arrow, and Colnaghi is of a similar standard. Close to a large painted yellow spot are a number of newer spit-protected routes (often with names painted below). These include **Have a Nice Day** and **Femmine in Gabbia** (both 5c/6a).

Just over 100m left, an obvious triangular overhang can be seen about 120m up. Taveggia starts below this, just to the right of some red writing at about 40/50m. 25 minutes.

Taveggia   285m E2 5c
Nardella, Marini & Pedroni 12/68

Despite the grassy nature of the first 2 pitches, an enjoyable route on generally good rock, with excellent in-situ protection where it is most needed.

Start by scrambling up to the right of a clean pillar to belay on a good ledge (peg low down).

1.   40m. Easily up grassy slabs and corners to the foot of a steep corner.

2.   30m 5a. Up the corner with a harder section to pass 2 pegs, to belay above a tree.

3.   20m 4b. Up slightly leftwards to belay below a clean corner beneath the left side of the triangular roof.

4.   25m 5a. Climb this enjoyably to belay left of the roof.

5.   20m. Easily up freshly scarred rock to a terrace - stance on the right with 2 large pegs. (It is possible to escape rightwards along the terrace from here.)

6.   20m 4b. Easily up to a stance beneath an obvious black niche (pegs).

7.   30m 5c. Enter the black niche and make hard bridging moves to overcome the roof. Continue steeply to a good ledge.

8.   20m 4a. Traverse right for 7/8m along a ledge, and go up to a peg and nut belay.

9.   25m 5a/b. Ignoring the superb slab on the right, make a hard move onto the wall above the stance and move left to a large ring-peg. Continue leftwards into a corner and, despite its vegetated appearance, climb this steeply to a stance and pegs.

10.   35m 5a. Continue up fine corners to exit right at trees. Belay on the right.

11.   20m. Easily up the gully to belay at the beginning of the descent path.

Descent

Follow the path back and right until it begins to drop down on the north side of the crag - fixed wire ropes. Eventually the path veers right and brings you back to the right-hand end of the crag. 20 minutes.

The red writing left of the start of Taveggia indicates the line of cracks and corners of **Anniversario** (330m 5b/A0, Uboldi & Borghi '86). Mainly VS/HVS climbing, with several pitches using points of aid, it is said to be worthwhile.

Fifty metres to the left on a detached pillar is a large yellow spot indicating the start of **Formica** (250m 5a/A1/2 or 6a/b), one of the hardest routes on Medale, and with some poor pegs. About 30m left of this and just right of the centre of the face is the classic:

Via Cassin   360m HVS 5a (4b/A0)
    Cassin & Dell'Oro '31

Starting below a ramp running upwards from right to left, the route is easy to follow due to the polish acquired during an estimated 10,000+ ascents! Most of the climbing is Severe/H.Severe, with a section of 4c at the beginning of the corner of P.3, a 5a traverse on P.5, and the celebrated leftward 'Traversino' from the cave of the 7th stance (4c/5a and said to be Robin Cousins' favourite pitch). All these pitches can be (and usually are) climbed on in-situ aid. Reputedly the most famous and popular limestone climb in the entire Alps, the whole route has been recently re-equipped. N.B. Traversing leftwards from the foot of Taveggia is difficult, and it is best to approach the Cassin route from below.

Gogna-Cerruti   245m E5 6b (E2 5b/A1)
    Gogna & Cerruti 17/5/69

A sustained and varied route consisting of strenuous climbing up a series of cracks and corners. Climbed free, the sixth pitch is much harder than anything else on the route. Care required with some of the in-situ pegs.

Approach

As for Taveggia to the first stone fence, then follow signs for the via ferrata, i.e. turn right at the fence, then left above it. Follow the fence until the path turns uphill to the foot of the rocks and the start of the via ferrata - marked with 2 large yellow spots painted on the rock. Follow steel ropes and spikes up steep, broken rocks for about 200m to reach a large rightward sloping terrace.

From the top of the ferrata descend rightwards under the rocks to a flared corner below a reddish overhang, which arches to the right at about 90 metres. Allow at least an hour.

1.   35m 5a. Follow the corner, first obliquely right, then up until a rightward traverse leads across a slab to a ledge.

2.   30m 5c/6a (5a/A1). Go up to a corner, climb this and move right. Continue more or less direct to a restricted stance.

3.   25m 4c. Up a short corner then diagonally rightwards to a sloping ledge. Directly up the grey arête to another ledge and belay.

4.   30m 5c (5a/A0). Move a few metres left and climb the overhang. Follow a long corner and a crack moving left to another restricted stance beneath a corner.

5.   25m 5c (5b/A1). The corner ovrhangs at first - follow this to a hanging stance below a smooth wall.

6.   30m 6b (5a/A1). Move up, then leftwards to the foot of a peg-bolt ladder. Follow this to a roof and traverse left below this to a stance beneath a grey corner.

7.   20m 5a. Climb the corner to a ledge.

8.   50m 5b. Move along the ledge to the left, and climb the white arête followed by a corner and overhang to reach a ledge. Move left and climb corners and slabs, gradually easing to the top.

Descent

From the summit cross, follow a path rightwards (N.E.) to meet the descent path as described for Taveggia. 30 minutes.

Some way left of the start of the Gogna-Cerruti is the start of **Breakdance**, left again the **Bonatti** (starting at a corner behind a tree). Worthwhile climbs on sound rock, with good pegs.

ANTIMEDALE

Approach and Character

This is the subsidiary cliff to the left of Medale. Access is as for the Via Gogna on Medale as far as the Via Ferrata. From there continue leftwards until a diagonal path leads up and right, eventually climbing steep scree to the foot of Antimedale. 1 hour.

Development of this pocketed sheet of excellent grey limestone began in 1984, with Ballerini and Dallona particularly prominent. The routes are generally short and technical, and have all been well-equipped with spits from abseil. At Bank Holidays and busy weekends it may be advisable to wear a helmet as there is danger

ANTIMEDALE
S.W.FACE -Lower Section

Beware falling stones

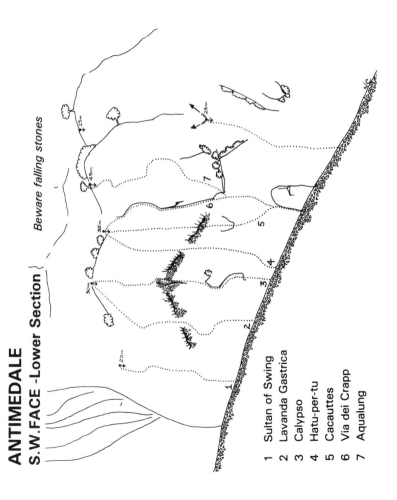

1 Sultan of Swing
2 Lavanda Gastrica
3 Calypso
4 Hatu-per-tu
5 Cacauttes
6 Via dei Crapp
7 Aqualung

of stone-fall from parties descending from the longer routes to the right - this applies especially to routes right of Cacauettes/Aqualung.

Descent
The descent from all the routes described here is by abseil.

The slab is bounded on the left by a bulging pillar, 5m right of this is a broken crack leading to a clean strip of rock between 2 vertical black stripes. This is **Sultan of Swing** 25m E2 5c (Bonfanti 30/12/84). Just right is **Lavanda Gastrica** E5 6b/c (Dallona '84).

Calypso 30m E2 5c
Ballerini & Bonfanti '84

This superb route starts just left of a curving flake 5m right and just above ground level. Climb directly past the black tufa pillar at the apex of the overlap above.

Hatu-Per-Tu 30m 6c/7a
Dallona 3/85

The hardest route on the crag starts at the base of a flake to the right, moving right before climbing the wall direct.

Three routes start up a crack to the right:
Cacauettes 30m E4 6a/b (Ballerini & Crotta '84). Start up the crack, move left and climb the wall right of Hatu. Excellent climbing said to be reminiscent of the first pitch of Mangoustine Scatophage.

Via dei Crapp (35m E2 5c) climbs the crack then bears left to climb the continuation crack, whereas **Aqualung**(42m E4 6a/b) breaks out right at this point.

Several routes go up to chains at a ledge above and right, with variation finishes from 5c to 6b. Further right the base of the crag drops away, and 2 longer climbs take the slabs right of a broken area of rock with a large (often wet) black stalactite at its foot.

Delta di Venere 60m E2/3 5c/6a
Dallona et al 8/12/84

Starts at a fig bush on a small ledge about 4m up, and just right and below a dead tree. (1) 20m 5c/6a. (2) 35m 5c/6a. Abseil off or climb another pitch of 5c.

Pello di Daino 75m E2 5c
(Dinoia et al 22/11/81)

Starts 4m right at bushes below a thin crack and reaches the second stance of the above by 2 pitches of 35m 5a, and 30m 5c.

N.B. From the third stance of both the above it is possible to continue to the terrace above Antimedale by 2 pitches (40m 5a, and 50m 4c). Descent is then by a cairned path to the left (west). *Particular care necessary to avoid dislodging stones onto those below.*

CORNO DEL NIBBIO

Approach

From Lecco follow signs for Val Sassina past the turning for Medale to Ballabio (about 5 miles from Lecco). Turn left as you enter the village and follow signs for Piani Resinelli, about 4 miles up steeply winding roads. Piani Resinelli is a plateau with a large parking area and shops to serve both the numerous day-trippers who flock to the mini-Dolomites of the Grignetta every summer weekend, and the rifugios and camping/caravan site which lie nearby. Nibbio is the fine rock tower easily visible to the NE from P. Resinelli. The older routes were almost all originally artificial, as this was once the training ground of the famous 'Spiders of Lecco' who were responsible for so many classic routes in the Dolomites and elsewhere.

From P. Resinelli take the road signed for the Rifugio SEM Cavalleti. A track soon leads off to the right past houses, narrowing to a path leading to the crag. At quiet times there are a few parking spaces in the side of the road near the beginning of the track, but at busy times it is necessary to park at Piani Resinelli. 15 minutes from there, or 5 from the beginning of the track. It is also possible to park on the road just under a mile before P. Resinelli. Park near a farm and walk uphill to the crag - 5 minutes.

Character

All the routes lie on the impending wall of the NE face, which provides an excellent refuge from summer heat, as well as the best hard climbing in the Lecco area. Slightly off vertical to the left, the great yellow and black striped wall becomes progressively steeper to the right, although as with Higgar Tor the eye refuses to recognize the true angle of the climbs on this section, (a stone falling from the top lands 7 or 8 metres out from the foot of the cliff). About half-way along the face is a 10m high detached pinnacle, and good bouldering is to be found on a number of other large boulders nearby. The climbs are well protected by bolts and

CORNO DEL NIBBIO
N.E.FACE

1 Bo Derek
2 Rupe Tarpea
3 Via Boga
4 Astro Boy
5 Quo Vadis
6 Sant 'Elia
7 Via Ratti
8 Via Cassin

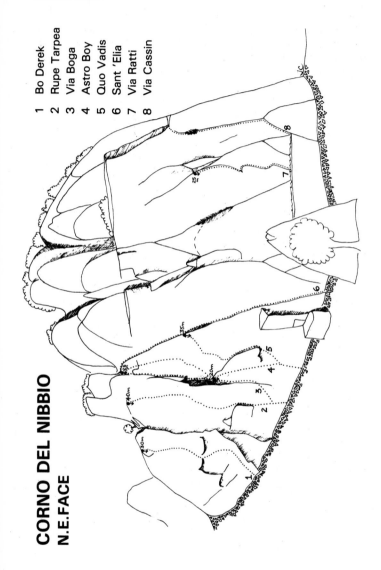

pegs, with chains for belays and abseils.

To the extreme left is a smaller buttress which is divided from the main cliff by the large chimney of **Camino Pellizari** (40m VS). Although of slightly scruffy appearance, the buttress gives an excellent well protected climb, and a good warm-up for the harder routes.

Bo Derek   30m E2 5b. (Ballerini autumn '82).

Rupe Tarpea   40m E3 5c
   Ballerini '82

Takes the clean wall to the right, starting at the left edge of a flake below a vertical line of holes. With the first bolt at 7m, a Friend is useful at the start.

The obvious corner to the right is:
Via Boga   50m E1 5b
Dell'Oro & Tizzoni 27/5/34

Start direct, or traverse in from the foot of the previous route. A strenuous and sustained route with many pegs, some of which are in poor condition but can be backed-up with nuts. A fine single pitch which may be split at 20m.

Then wall right is broken by a ledge curving up from the right to join Boga at 20m. Starting 5m right of Boga at a crack is the superb:
Astro Boy   55m E4 6a
   Ballerini & Magni '83
1.   20m 6a. Up then diagonally left to belay as for Boga.
2.   35m 6a. Cross the superb wall diagonally rightwards, then follow a crack back left to the top stance of Boga.

Starting as the above, but moving diagonally rightwards across the ledge to the first stance of Sant'Elia, is the less sustained **Quo Vadis**   35m E3 6a. (Ballerini & Crotta '84).

Just right is **Spit and Span**, a direct on Quo Vadis (7a).

Sant'Elia   80m E5 6b, 6a
   Molteni et al 1934

The obvious oblique right-left crack has been gradually freed, and recently equipped with spits.

Just right of the pinnacle is a ledge at 5m (huge belay bolt on ledge). The innocuous looking crack/groove system above gives an extremely strenuous but well protected pitch: **Via Ratti**   25m E2 5b. (Ratti et al 8/35).

The unattractive crack to the right is the original start to Ratti, whereas the Cassin route takes the polished crack further right (5b with variation starts from Severe to 5c/6a). The more broken north face around to the right has a number of climbs in the V.Diff. to Severe grades.

SASSO D'INTROBIO

Follow the main Val Sassina road for just over 5 miles after Ballabio to a point where the road makes a sharp right turn over a river. A lane leads off right to parking beneath the crag, which is easily visible from the road.

Despite its scruffy appearance the crag offers good climbing on solid rock, and its quick drying SE exposure combined with what must be the ultimate in ease of access make it a useful choice for a short or wet day. It contains ten bolt-protected routes of from 30 to 60 metres. Mostly in the 5c/6a range with names painted below, these include from left to right: **Paola VII**   6a and **Paola VI** 5c. 35m. Two variants with a common start and finish - abseil off.

Via Centrale   35m 5b. Abseil off or continue by;

Incubo Motopsichico   30m 6a. (perhaps the best pitch here).

Francesca   55m 5a, 5b. A classic with an excellent variant first pitch: **Oltre il Tramonto**   25m 5c. (The indirect start from the left is 6b/7a.)

The slabs amongst the trees on the opposite side of the road bear a number of climbs, but there are some access problems.

BASTIONATA DEL LAGO

Pilastro Rosso (Panziera-Riva)   205m E3 6a
   Panzieri, Riva & Passerini 5/75

The Bastionata del Lago is the steep area of rock above the Lecco-Colico road. Despite the rather uninspiring approach, and the proximity of the busy road below, this steep line up an imposing reddish pillar offers an impressive challenge on excellent rock, and is probably the best route of the area. There are now a number of short bolt protected routes to be found about 200m to the right of this. Varying from 5c to 6b/c, they are mostly the work of Marco Ballerini.

Approach

Driving north towards Colico on the lakeside road from Lecco, it is about one and a half miles to the first possible turn-off on the right. Turn off under the railway arches to park - parking alongside the road may result in your car being towed away. Return to the road and take the path under the arch, through a clump of *buddleias* and past the end of a fence to a steep gully, with a fixed rope on the final section. The path then trends to the right - take the fork leading directly up large scree to a vertical reddish pillar, defined on the left by a steep vegetated area, and on the right by a smaller white buttress. 15 minutes.

Start just right of centre where stepped rocks lead up and leftwards.

1.   35m 6a. Follow rock steps diagonally leftwards to a horizontal ledge. Strenuous jamming leads up the wide vertical crack on the right.

2.   35m 5c. Climb the crack, with a deviation onto the left wall just before it becomes a chimney. Move into the chimney and climb this and the ensuing corner to a ledge on the right.

3.   30m 5a. Move up a little, then diagonally left to a small ledge.

4.   30m 4c. Diagonally right to overcome a short wall, then horizontally left to a small ledge below a long corner.

5.   25m 5c. Climb the corner.

6.   30m 5b/c. Follow a crack up the wall above, then traverse left to gain another vertical crack and follow this over slightly vegetated rock to the base of an evil-looking chimney.

7.   20m 5a. Climb the chimney to trees and the end of the difficulties.

Descent

Go right (south) and descend a grassy ramp. Make a 30m abseil into the gully delineating the pillar on the right. Another abseil of 35m leads to a ledge which is followed to the left (north). Another 2 abseils of 45 and 50m return you to the foot of the pillar.

TORRIONE DI VAL REALBA

The combination of very easy access, excellent rock and sunny aspect, make this a particularly good crag for the middle grade climber. The two VS are superb, and with an E3, and E4 and a number of variants it would also give a worthwhile day for the harder climber. All the climbs are spit-protected although it is worth carrying a few nuts - particularly on the VS.

Approach

Drive N towards Colico on the lakeside road (as for Bastionata del Lago) for about three and a half miles, until you see a green Moto Guzzi building on the lakeside just before Abbadia Lariana. The crag can be seen above the trees on the opposite side of the road, with parking just beyond. Walk a little towards Lecco and turn left into an underpass beneath the railway. Follow a path for 10 minutes, with a steep scramble to the foot of the tower.

The slabs at the base are split by 2 obvious, rather vegetated diagonal cracks going from right to left. The easiest route on the crag, the **Via Normale**(V.Diff.), follows the left-hand crack for about 30m to a ledge, takes a crack from the left end of this to another ledge, before traversing almost horizontally rightwards to finish as the variant last pitch of Buita.

Diedro del Buita   70m VS 4c

An excellent route on superb rock.

1.   30m 4c. Climb the slab left of the crack of the Via Normale past 2 bolts and a peg to join the crack at about 17m. Continue in the line of the crack to a stance below a superb layback flake.

2.   15m 4c. Climb the flake to the ledge below the upper wall.

3.   Either: (a) use several peg-bolts for aid to climb the slab above (4c). Or: (b) walk across to the extreme right of the ledge and climb up near the arête (2 pegs), then follow the crack leading slightly leftwards - slightly friable rock, medium nuts necessary for protection. Or: (c) abseil off from chains.

Morlach's Shadow   E4 6b+

Zanetti 11/84

A rather disjointed line starting with extremely thin, but well protected slab climbing near the right arête, followed by a very easy 20m to belay on a ledge by a tree. The second pitch takes either of the bolt lines above the final ledge on excellent rock (6a/b).

Descent

For either of the above, abseil off from chains.

Rif-Raf   55m E3 6a

Casari, Comin & Rossetti 31/12/84

Scramble up to the right of the tower to another section of very clean rock, slightly higher but immediately adjacent.

1.   35m 5a. Climb the slab on the left past a bolt and thread to the overhang above (possible belay).

Easily over this and up to a ledge with peg and nut belay.

Torrione di Val Realba. Diedro del Buita.   167

2.   20m 6a. The line of bolts up the slab above.

(An enjoyable, and easier variation is to do pitch 1 in combination with pitch 2 of Lama.)

Via della Lama   55m VS 4c

1.   25m 4b. Climb the corner right of the above, starting by the slab, to belay at a tree on the ledge.

2.   30m 4c (with perhaps 1 move of 5a). Up the cracks above to a fine layback flake - climb this to a difficult exit. Tree belay.

Descent

For the two climbs above it is possible to abseil from a tree, but as the ropes are likely to become jammed it is better to walk off to the right (facing in). Fixed rope for the first stage of the descent.

MELLO AND THE VALTELLINA

Val di Mello is one of the most beautiful valleys in Europe, and every climber should visit it at least once. Despite its fame it remains relatively undeveloped both in terms of climbing and tourism, and this is the key to much of its attraction. The waterfalls spilling over the side-valleys into the clear pools of the river, the flickering butterflies, grasshoppers and crickets, the hanging woods of beech, whitebeam, ash and fir that clothe the hillsides, the numerous boulders with their innumerable problems, the silver granite slabs and walls, the ever-changing backdrop of cloud-shadow and the sun upon Monte Disgrazia - all these make Mello a place to be experienced, rather than just another place to climb.

Despite the acres of climbable rock, the 73 routes described in the latest ('85) guidebook compare with 43 in the original 1980 guide to reflect an incredibly slow pace of development. This is principally because of the local climbers' distaste for bolts, and although a few spit-equipped routes have appeared in the last two years, these have been largely the work of 'outsiders' and it will be interesting to see if these survive. The valley's reputation for thin slab climbs with minimal or non-existent protection is largely due to Antonio Boscacci, and his new routes on Piede dell'Elefante are firmly in that tradition. However, it was some time before standards of crack-climbing reached the same level of expertise, and for some time comparatively straightforward cracks continued to be climbed on aid, leaving many cracks fairly bristling with pegs. However, a normal granite rack of nuts, Friends and tie-offs should be carried for the longer routes.

The best climbing is to be found on the long classics such as Kundalini, Luna Nascente, and Oceano Irrazionale, although there are enough short, easily accessible routes for easier days. The rock is rarely less than perfect and the bouldering possibilities virtually endless, with a guide available purely for bouldering. Lying in the rain-shadow of the Bregaglia, the weather compares favourably with other granite areas such as Handegg, and the predominantly

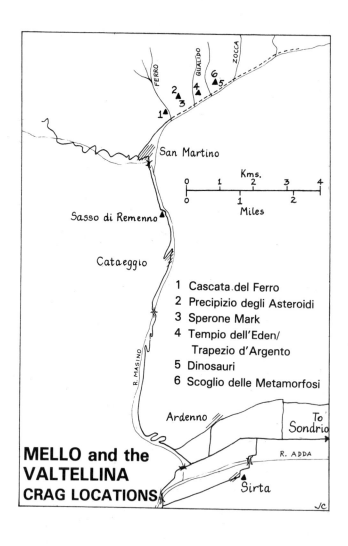

1 Cascata del Ferro
2 Precipizio degli Asteroidi
3 Sperone Mark
4 Tempio dell'Eden/
  Trapezio d'Argento
5 Dinosauri
6 Scoglio delle Metamorfosi

**MELLO and the
VALTELLINA
CRAG LOCATIONS**

south-facing crags dry quickly after rain. However, the nearby areas of Sasso di Remenno and Sirta offer short, well protected outcrop climbs, that are often dry even when Mello is lost in clouds. The climbing season extends from April to October, although the nature of the valley ensures that climbing days are very short towards either extreme, and the best months are July to September.

Access, Camping etc.

The western end of the main valley of the Valtellina is approached from Zurich via Chur - Splugen Pass - Chiavenna; or from Milan via Lecco and the slow grind around the shores of Lake Como. It is also possible to enter the Valtellina further east via the Bernina Pass - particularly useful to alpinists climbing in the Bernina and Engadine areas. Driving east along the Valtellina towards Sondrio, a small turning goes left for Cataeggio at Ardenno, a few kilometres after Morbegno. Follow this for about 10 miles to reach San Martino (passing the enormous boulder of Sasso Remenno just before the village). Go through the village and continue bearing right for Mello (the fork bearing left leads up a good road to the Val di Bagni which offer an alternative camping area). The road soons deteriorates into a track (which improves after 2 bad sections) and continues to a large parking area at the mouth of the valley. Just beyond this is the bar of Gatto Rosso, and all approaches are described from here. A footbridge leads to the opposite side of the river and ample camping possibilities. There have been some cases of thefts from cars - particularly at weekends - so you may prefer to camp near your vehicle in the fenced area towards Gatto Rosso. In either case the charges are very cheap - only about a pound per day in 1986. Camping is also possible in many quiet positions further up the valley, although care should be taken to avoid camping on hay meadows.

A limited menu is available at Gatto Rosso, and there are restaurants, bars and shops in San Martino, including a climbing shop with guides, chalk and all the other necessities of life.

Guidebooks

Val di Mello - 9,000 Metri Sopra i Prati (i.e. 9,000m of Climbing above the Meadows) - Masa & Merrizi, pub. Egeria 1985.

(Earlier and much cheaper guidebooks by Boscacci and Guerini are still available.)

Sasso di Remenno - Boscacci 1985 (contains over 70 routes on

Remenno and neighbouring crags).
Strutture di Valtellina - Miotti & Mottarella 1981. (Outcrops in
the Valtellina including Remenno and the only guide to Sirta.)

CASCATA DEL FERRO

This is the obvious waterfall more or less opposite the campsite,
well to the left of the base of Asteroidi. Several routes take the
slabs on either side of the lowest torrent.

Approach
Follow the right bank of the stream up to the foot of the falls. 5
minutes. This is normally very easy, but in late August 1986 the
whole area between the track and falls was a morass of mud over
a 2 metre layer of old snow - the result of an avalanche the
previous winter. 10 minutes.

Just right of the waterfall is:

Mixomeceto   30m E1 5c
Gogna, Guerini, Merizzi & Moitti 17/7/77

An easy slab leads to an obvious traverse line diagonally leftwards
beneath a flake. Climb this past peg runners until very close to the
waterfall, then follow an easy groove up to a stance.

A second pitch continues for another 50m at about V.Diff.
standard, but it is easier to walk off to the right.

Index   30m E2 5b
Boscacci (solo) '78

Start a few metres right in Mixomeceto, to the left of a vegetated
corner. Scramble up onto a ledge and climb the slab above
completely without protection. Crux at about 7m, after which the
angle eases. A scratched arrow indicates the start.

Lo Scivolo (The Slide)   60m E4 6b
Swiss Team 8/84

Starting just left of the waterfall, climb up to a ledge and overlap.
Very thin friction climbing leads up the slab above. With 4 bolts in
place it is now a much less serious proposition.

Via Gossemberg (300m Severe) starts left of Scivolo to take a
wandering line up slabs, ledges and vegetation to the left of the
waterfall.

Al Churcher on Diedro di Popi E4 6b - Sasso di Remenno, Mello.
Photo: Jill Churcher.

PRECIPIZIO DEGLI ASTEROIDI

Standing high above Gatto Rosso, and dominating the lower part of the valley, Il Precipizio is the 'El Cap' of Mello. It is defined high on the left by the Val Livincina, which becomes a wooded gully lower down. This normally carries little more than a stream, but after heavy rain it becomes a raging torrent. The cliff is divided roughly into halves by a tree-covered terrace running diagonally upwards from left to right - the Great Ledge - and the name Precipizio really applies only to the face above this terrace. Roughly in the centre of this face is a nose formed by a large vertical pillar, and our climb takes the obvious crack system defining the right-hand side of this.

The line up the left-hand side is **Bodenshaff** (Maddonna and Merizzi 1979). Originally climbed with aid, including a pitch of A3, it was freed by Bassi and Pedrini in 1986 at 6a/b.

Approach

From Gatto Rosso follow the bed of the stream (normally dry) up the Val Livincina, to reach a waterfall at the foot of the rocks - 30 minutes. Go left of this by steep grass and broken rock to the base of an overhanging wall split by a chimney corner - its base hidden by a large beech tree. Climb the chimney (bolt runner), or if wet the grassy crack to the right (4a to 4c). Continue up through steep woods, surmounting a steep section with the aid of a metal spike. On reaching the top of a small promontory, follow a fixed rope along an exposed 'path' overlooking the stream until you reach its bed. A narrow path climbs up the opposite side onto the Great Ledge - follow this for about 200m to a point right of the obvious striking crackline.

Allow at least 2 hours - rope required!

Descent (E5?)

From the summit of the crag follow sloping grassy terraces diagonally rightwards, using frequent abseils to reach the nearest branch of the gully. Make one abseil from pegs, then traverse rightwards to make a 50m abseil from a tree into the main gully. Follow this (very wet after rain) making many abseils from anchors which are often difficult to find. Arriving at a level area above a very steep and imposing section, look for a cairn on the left which marks a

Precipizio degli Asteroidi
Oceano Irrazionale 500m E4 6a

footpath which almost immediately rises over vegetated steps to reach the foot of a smooth slab. Follow a 'path' below this, which soon descends through the trees to rejoin the Great Ledge. (At least 3 hours.)

Oceano Irrazionale   500m E3 5c
Guerini & Villa 7/77

The combination of length and seriousness of approach and descent, with the strenuous nature of much of the 500 metres of climbing (sometimes with spaced protection), results in an unusually committing and demanding route. It is best approached in the spirit of an adventure rather than as just another climb, for in the words of one climber: 'Half the attraction of the route is the fun you can have finding it!'. Certainly worthwhile for its superb position and atmosphere. 50m ropes essential, and a good selection of Friends and nuts for both protection and belays.

Start where a large detached flake forms a chimney with the main wall, some 40m right of the obvious crack-line.

1.   20m 4c. Climb the chimney, exiting onto the edge of the flake and follow this rightward. Traverse horizontally left to a peg belay.

2.   35m 5c. Climb a short steep wall to two small spikes, making a descending leftwards traverse from the second of these to an obvious ramp-line. A rising traverse over rock and vegetation leads to the foot of a large, vertical crack.

3.   45m 4c/5a. Climb the crack to join a second parallel crack and a niche - peg belays.

4.   50m 5b. Continue by either the left or right-hand branch at roughly the same standard to a stance in a niche.

5.   35m 5c. Climb directly up the awkward crack to beneath the large roof. Difficult off-width climbing leads diagonally rightwards to a small cave at the end of the roof.

6.   10m 5b. Exit rightwards by a crack to reach a fir tree.

7.   50m. From the second tree, traverse left to the foot of a long corner. Go up this to a grass ledge.

8/9.   90m 4a. Continue up the corner.

10/11.   90m 4c. The corner becomes a crack behind a leaning flake, climb the flake.

12.   Either continue direct (4b), or more easily diagonally rightwards to a large larch tree. Follow steep vegetation back leftwards to reach the summit.

SPERONE MARK

This slabby buttress immediately below Asteroidi has a number of indifferent routes and one worthwhile crack climb - particularly valuable as it 'goes' even during heavy rain.

Approach
Take the main path past Gatto Rosso to the next building, and follow the path on its left through a tiny hamlet (note the building growing out of the rock). Bear right, then finally left - the route is hidden in a cave-like recess behind a group of ash and sycamore trees.

Giallo Ocra 40m E1 5b
  Neri (solo) 6/78
Cracks and flakes lead in an obvious diagonal line to the roof on the right. If wet lower off from pegs below the roof, otherwise pull round the roof and go up a short slab to a tree belay. Abseil off.

TEMPIO DELL'EDEN/TRAPEZIO D'ARGENTO

The upper cliff of Tempio dell'Eden with its huge left to right diagonal roof (the line of L'Alba del Nirvana) is separated from the lower slabs of Trapezio d'Argento by a wooded terrace which becomes a steep gully on the left-hand side.

Approach
Follow the path upstream from Gatto Rosso, crossing a tributary on stepping stones. Turn left off the path after a short rise (i.e. just before a bridge crossing the river to houses), and follow a way-marked path (red squares) which leads diagonally up to the left-hand end of Trapezio.

L'Alba del Nirvana 155m HVS 5a
  Gossemberg & Guerini 5/76
1. 35m 4c. Direct up the smooth slab on the left-hand side of Trapezio d'Argento to belay on the terrace. Unprotected until small flake at 20m. (This is Stomaco Peloso - the original start is by the gully further left.)
2. 15m. To a tree below the upper slab.
3. 40m 4c. Go up a little, traverse diagonally left and then return rightwards to a stance below the huge roof (or climb more or less

Tempo dell'Eden / Trapezio d'Argento
1 - *L'Alba del Nirvana 155m HVS 5a*
2 - *Nuova Dimensione 135m E2 5b*

direct to this point via a bolt runner).

4.   20m 5a. A steep crack leads to easier climbing along the top of a large flake. It is also possible to traverse below the flake at a similar standard. (The alarmingly overhanging crack above is La Signora del Tempo, 6b).

5.   45m 4b. Continue to the end of the roof.

Descent

Climb or abseil down rightwards to a large pine tree, from where a 20m abseil leads to the wooded terrace. Descend the gully on its left (facing in), avoiding a steepening by a short abseil to rejoin the foot of the cliff just left of the starting slab. The overhanging crack to the right of the final stance gives a good jamming pitch (12m E1 5b).

Nuova Dimensione   135m E2 5b
   Boscacci & Merizzi 5/77

Once one of the most famous climbs in Italy and its first grade 7, today it is something of a 'soft touch' at the grade. However with the crux well above protection and the roof waiting below, it still requires a cool head. None of the pitches are well protected, but carry a few small nuts.

   Towards the right-hand end of Trapezio d'Argento is a low horizontal roof. Start below the right end of this.

1.   45m 5a. Climb up to the roof and make a long leftward traverse to a stance and pegs.

2.   45m 5b. Climb diagonally rightwards to reach a vein. Move up this until a step right across a small corner brings pegs within reach, and a sigh of relief. Traverse right to a flake and belay.

3.   45m 5a. Up the slab above to reach an overlap formed of two veins of rock. Traverse left along this, return right and up to the wooded terrace above. Descend as for Alba del Nirvana or abseil off further left (facing in).

   There are now several variant lines between the traverses of the first and second pitches, and a direct finish which climbs virtually direct up the slab above the first belay (**Steinbrecher**   6b).

SARCOFAGO

Situated to the left of the foot of Dinosauri on the opposite bank of the Cascata di Qualido, the name was suggested by a large detached flake said to resemble a sarcophagus.

Approach
As for Metamorfosi.

Il Cunicolo Acuto   80m VS 4c
   Guerini et al 13/8/75
As most of the route lies inside the crag it should perhaps be given a caving grade. An interesting climb requiring a wide variety of crack and chimney techniques.

   Start at a red arrow in a cave on the right side of the cliff.
1.   25m 4b. Climb the corner crack on the right of the cave, to belay in a niche left of the foot of the great flake of the Sarcofago.
2.   30m 4c. Up the vertical chimney to a stance with trees.
3.   25m 4b. Cracks lead to the top.

DINOSAURI (or Dimore degli Dei)

Approach
Follow the path from Gatto Rosso past the waymarked turnings for Tempio dell'Eden and Metamorfosi, to where a tributary stream comes in on the left just before the hamlet of Piana. Follow the path along the true left bank of the stream to a huge larch tree clearly visible from the main path. 10 minutes from the path, 25 minutes in all.

Il Risveglio di Kundalini   400m E1 5b/c
   Guerini & Villa 4/76
A long and varied classic, generally well protected, and on good rock, although liable to seepage under the arch after heavy rain. Kundalini itself is the best route of its standard in the valley, and by continuing up Luna Nascente one can experience over 2,000 feet of almost continuous climbing - only interrupted by a short walk through the beechwoods between the two routes. With its ease of access and non-alpine nature, the resulting combination is of a quality and length with few equals in Europe.

Start
Directly below the left-hand side of the huge arched roof which characterizes the upper part of Dinosauri, and which provides the substance of the route.

Descent
Walk left through the wood to meet a well-constructed path which returns you to the foot of the climb in 30 minutes.

Dinosauri / Scoglio delle Metamorfosi   1 - L'Albero delle Pere
2 - Il Risveglio di Kundalini   3 - Luna Nascente   4 - Polimago

1.   35m 4b. Follow the obvious traverse rightwards to a stance beneath a roof.

2.   40m 5b/c. Go up to the end of the roof and traverse delicately leftwards across a slab - crux move near the start (peg). Easier climbing continues left and then up a vegetated corner to the foot of the obvious jam-crack.

3.   40m 4c. The Serpent Crack. Climb this enjoyably, and with good protection from big nuts to its end.

4.   30m 5b. The thankfully short off-width, followed by a slabby wall to a wooded area.

5.   40m 5a. Climb the easy slab above, then a corner to reach the arch. Follow this rightwards to a niche.

   (If the arch is wet it is best to take a low traverse line from here, rejoining the original route at the 7th stance (4a, -, 4c).

6.   45m 4b. The crack under the arch leads to a beak formed of detached flakes. Descend diagonally rightwards to a shallow crack, traverse horizontally right, then up diagonally to a stance.

7.   45m 4c. Traverse more or less horizontally right by ledges and chickenheads (sparse protection), before moving diagonally upwards to belay on a ledge below an overlap.

8.   35m 4c. Go up to and over the overlap and continue traversing rightwards to a ledge and trees.

9.   40m 5b/c. Go right over exposed slabs, left to surmount an overlap, then back right around an arête and up a short corner before returning left to a stance. Care needed to avoid rope drag on this pitch.

10.   50m 4c. Follow slabs and corners right, and go up to belay at the edge of the beechwoods - The Bosco Incantato or Enchanted Wood.

   To continue via Luna Nascente walk left through the wood (facing in), then continue as described in the approach for that climb.

L'Albero delle Pere   265m E1 5b/c
   Boscacci & Merizzi 12/6/77

Three unpleasantly vegetated pitches lead to a superb upper section, culminating in the unforgettable slab of **Lucertole al Sole (Lizards of the Sun)**, 55m of superbly unprotected slab climbing on the edge of everything. Unmistakably a Boscacci route!

   Start left of Kundalini at a large tree just right of the waterfall.

1.   50m 5a. Climb vegetated slabs and ribs bearing generally right to trees (possible stance). Go slightly left through trees and

up to a slightly overhanging crack. Up this and through more trees to belay at the foot of a small chimney.

2.   35m 4b. Climb easy rock, then a small chimney and gully, finally traversing right to another tree belay.

3.   50m 5b. Up a vegetated chimney/gully, followed by trees and ledges. (possible belay.) Traverse slightly left and climb a chimney which becomes a crack. Escape delicately rightwards to a stance below an overhung niche.

4.   35m 5b/c. Over the overhang and up to a sloping ledge. Go left to a corner and follow this to a stance with 2 trees.

5.   40m 4b. Climb the slab diagonally rightwards to belay on nuts at a small flake.

6.   55m 4c. Tie both ropes together and pad more or less directly up the slab above - the angle gradually easing, but without protection - to belay on the edge of the Bosco Incantato.

(N.B. It is possible to avoid the top 2 pitches by climbing a grassy gully to the left of the fifth stance.)

Descent

As for Kundalini.

SCOGLIO DELLA METAMORFOSI

Approach

Follow the main path from Gatto Rosso past a good swimming hole with a large boulder to a flat green meadow with a slabby silver boulder. A waymarked path turns up to the left and zig-zags up the hillside past Sarcofago to cross the stream below a waterfall (15 minutes to here). The path continues to be waymarked up the other bank of the stream, with well-constructed sections of steps where it becomes steeper. On reaching the beechwood of the Bosco Incantato continue straight up to the foot of the rocks, turn left and go up a small slab then a gully to a higher wood below Metamorfosi. Start in a cave-like grotto on the extreme right. 1 hour.

Luna Nascente (The Rising Moon)   335m E2 5b

   Boscacci, Ghezzi & Milani 3/9/78

A wonderful climb taking the long corner system up the right-hand side of Metamorfosi - probably the finest climb at Mello.

1.   15m 5b (AO). Gain the horizontal flake at the back of the grotto by either: (a) bridging onto the flake behind, or (b) using 2 pegs for aid. Traverse leftwards along the flake to belay at the foot of the chimney of Polimago.

2. 15m 5b. Climb diagonally rightwards to the roof and traverse horizontally right beneath it (several pegs). Layback around the edge of the roof to gain the foot of the long diedre - hanging belay from pegs. It is possible to belay higher up the diedre, but this is likely to incur severe rope drag.

3/4/5. Climb the magnificent diedre by three superb pitches (25m, 40m, 30m), mostly at 5a with odd moves of 5b, to a stance below an obvious large niche topped by a roof (the Occhio di Falco - Eye of the Falcon).

6. 40m 5a. Bridge up to where the crack widens and traverse horizontally leftwards past a peg to reach a large hollow flake. Layback down this, traverse left and climb up the wide crack on the other side of the flake to a peg belay.

N.B. Leave one rope free from the start of the traverse to protect the second. It is also possible to climb direct to this point (5c), but this avoids a unique and enjoyable part of the climb.

7. 50m 4b. Continue up the wide crack with little protection to a peg and dead tree belay.

8. 50m. Make a long easy leftwards traverse, following an obvious felspar vein to the foot of a short crack.

9. 25m 4c. Up the crack trending right, then the slab above to grass and a belay on juniper bushes.

10. 45m. Walk left along a felspar band, and go up an easy scoop in a slab to belay on a large tree.

Polimago (360m E2 5b. Masa & Merizzi 28/5/79) continues up the chimney above the first stance of Luna Nascente, to belay on top of the large flake forming the left wall of the chimney (55m 5b, 4b). Friction climbing up steep then easier angled slabs leads first direct, then rightwards to an arch, from where a rightward line follows slabs and cracks to rejoin Luna Nascente at the sixth stance, (115m 5a, 4c, 5b). Said to be almost the equal of Luna Nascente in quality, although less well protected.

Descent

Go up through trees and bilberries, passing a dome of rock on the left to reach old stone walls. Follow these to 2 vertical stones forming a gateway. Descend vegetated stone steps to enter a gully and continue down this to where it meets a second gully. Cross this by a rock step, traversing east around a spur until a path descends into the second gully. Follow a path near a stream - often through heavy undergrowth and bog - until it reaches the beech-woods. Bear back west (right when facing the valley) through the woods to reach the main gully bounding the east side of Metamorfosi, and cross this to return to the foot of the climb.

It is also possible to descend by abseil from trees to the east of Luna Nascente (i.e. to the left when facing the valley).

SASSO DI REMENNO

Once described as the largest boulder in the entire Alps, this 50 metre high mass of granitoide lies next to the road just outside San Martino - in fact part of it was dynamited away to allow the passage of the road. Parking is available on the opposite side of the road, and beneath the artificial routes on the vertical roadside face (weekend assaults on these bolt ladders frequently result in traffic jams of incredulous tourists).

Most routes described here were the work of Miotti and are protected with peg-bolts, with the most recent ('85 onwards) having spits. However, some upper sections are quite sparsely protected and Friends are useful here. There are 4 distinct faces and the routes are described in an anti-clockwise direction from the road.

THE WEST FACE

A path leads up the gully to the right of the N (i.e. roadside face), and two vertical cracks are clearly visible, with a common start up the flake crack below.

Balconi Fioriti   5c 40m. is the lefthand.

Fessura di Budino   5b 40m (Panzeri '79) to the right.

The Wall   6a/b (Cucchi '85) is a new route to the left.

Further right is a slabby bay which gives a good V.Diff:

Via Comune   40m

Starts 3m right of the corner. Climb up to small ledges leading rightwards, then up to a large ledge and possible belay. Go up the flake behind the ledge, then return left to the corner and layback up this.

Right of this the ground drops away beneath an obvious flake, this is:

Via della Lama   50m E1 5b
   Miotti & Bottani

Flakes and grooves lead up the arête to finish left of the fine easy crack at the top. Climbing the crack reduces the standard to HVS. Spaced protection near the top - medium/large Friends useful for pockets.

SASSO DI REMENNO

WEST FACE

1 Fessura di Budino
2 Via Comune
3 Via della Lama

SASSO DI REMENNO   SOUTH FACE

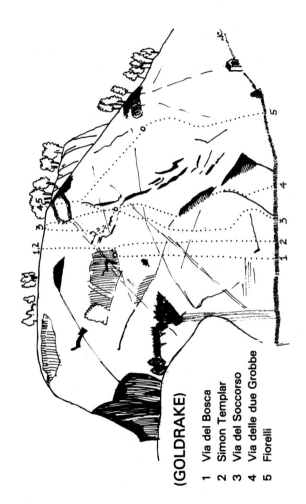

(GOLDRAKE)

1   Via del Bosca
2   Simon Templar
3   Via del Soccorso
4   Via delle due Grobbe
5   Fiorelli

187

Koscierlitz is a direct start (6a) and **Diedro di Popi** E4 6b, follows the corner throughout, with a poorly protected start. The ground drops away steeply to the right, and several new routes are visible up the bulging wall above.

THE SOUTH FACE

A favourite bouldering area with a good grassy landing, the traverse is often crowded and can be followed at a variety of standards from 4b to 6b, depending on the line. It is possible to camp below the face, and there is good spring water close at hand. The wall gives some of the most popular routes on the boulder, which are described from left to right.

Via del Bosca E2 5c/6a (Boscacci) and **Simon Templar** E1 5b (Cucchi), are new spit protected climbs.

Soccorso 55m E1 5b
Angelini & Bertarelli

Starts left of an obvious vein running from left to right. Climb the wall which soon becomes a ramp. Make a few moves up the vein then pull left to a small ledge. Follow bolts to a belay on the ledge above. Two exits lead from here:

(a) the original finish moves left to climb a pillar at 5b.

(b) The direct finish (E2 5c/6a Miotti) was originally artificial and is very well protected by peg-bolts.

Via delle due Gobbe 55m E1 5b
Gugiatti

Starts in the middle of the wall directly below the apex of an inverted 'V' formed by two ribs, and climbs directly up to the same belay ledge as Soccorso, before moving right to finish.

8m left of an old stone wall is:

Fiorelli 65m VS 4c
Up the crack into a large scoop - move left onto a rib and climb this to a ledge and belay. Follow flakes right, then a slab back left to a final diagonal corner. (There are a number of variants on this.)

The overhanging face of the boulder opposite (known as Goldrake) has a number of short hard climbs (6a to 7a).

The East Face of Remenno has a shrine at its foot, with a block to is right. **Olga Pigolza** (HVS/E1 5a Boscacci) climbs the diagonal rib on the right, then the slab above past two bolts.

Returning to the North Face above the road, the obvious flake going left is taken by **L'ama Follemente** E2 5c (Cucchi).

PIEDE DELL'ELEFANTE

There are a number of routes on the other boulders in the area, but the friction climbs of this superb slab are in sharp contrast to those described above. Looking across the road from Remenno to the hillside opposite, the Elefante is the silvery slab criss-crossed with white quartz veins. About 10 minutes from the road.

Crazy Horse   90m E2 5b
  Miotti & Mottarella '78

The classic of the slab starts from a grassy ledge reached by scrambling up and left from the foot of the crag. Delicate and poorly protected.
1. 40m 5a. Follow the white vein diagonally rightwards to another ledge. Small wire just before half-way.
2. 50m 5b. Fairly direct up the slab above, keeping left of black streaks - 2 bolts (although there are rumours that these have been chopped). Descend to the right (facing in).

Two new Boscacci routes **Cipria**   5c, and **Elmesbrisigalpe** also 5c, take lines to the left and right respectively. Both completely without protection.

SIRTA

Described in Miotti's *Strutture di Valtellina* as a 'little piece of England in Italy', La Caürga di Sirta rises steeply up behind the village of Sirta and its domed church, and can be clearly seen from the main Valtellina road. As the original routes are a complexity of variant starts and finishes, those described below are a selection of the most logical combinations, and have been given the name of the principal pitch.

Access and Descent
From the point where the road from Mello meets the Valtellina, turn east towards Sondrio for a short distance before taking the first turning on the right. Park in the village square near the church, from where a well-constructed path leads past a bar to the foot of the crag - about 2 minutes. Scramble up and right from the top of the climbs, and descend to the right of the cliff.

The crag faces south-west, giving steep, sunny climbing on solid gneiss, with good protection from nuts and in-situ pegs. It has been reported that many of the peg-bolts have now been replaced by spits. Described from left to right.

LA CAÜRGA
DI SIRTA

1 Via C.L.
2 Presentimento d'Orologio
3 Fiorellini per Heidi

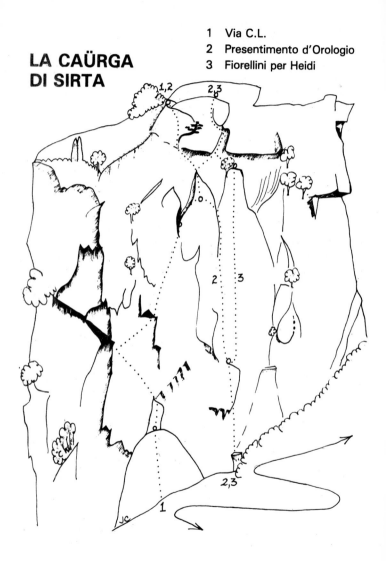

Via C.L.   80m E1 5b/c
   Arrigoni et al. FFA Merizzi & Miotti 6/77
Start on the left of the main face where the path meets the cliff at
the foot of an obvious slab.
1.   10m 4b. Climb the front of the slab to belay at the top (or
scramble up the ramp on the right).
2.   30m 5b. Climb onto the block above and traverse diagonally
leftwards almost to the arête at a point level with a large roof.
Return diagonally right and cross a small roof (crux) on the right
before following a crack above to belay in a large niche.
3.   10m 4c. Up the ramp to the right, and traverse horizontally
right to belay.
4.   30m 5c. Zig-zag up flakes to a pine tree, and go left to a steep
crack. Up this with one hard move.

Presentimento d'Orologio   80m E3 6a
   Miotti & Merizzi '78 (and '80 **Gorilla Lilla** start).
Scramble up right from the start of CL, to a square cut ledge just
below the point where the path curves back to the foot of the cliff.
1.   50m 6a. Climb the steep rib above the left end of the ledge to
a second ledge (possible belay). Continue up the scoop on the left
passing several pegs, and make hard moves left to reach a stance.
2.   30m Finish as for CL, or go up a little as for that route and take
the crack system further right (5b).

Fiorellini per Heidi   35m E4 6b
   Miotti & Merizzi '80
Start at the right-hand end of the second ledge of Presentimento,
either by that route or the ramp/corner further right.
1.   35m 6b. Climb the yellowish wall leftwards to a crack. Follow
this to a black corner leading leftwards to a peg-bolt. Make hard
moves past several more peg-bolts until it is possible to traverse
left to join the right-hand finish to Presentimento. (A more difficult
variant takes the scooped wall directly above the ledge - protected
only by peg-bolts which are reputed to be less than bomb-proof.)

   The continuation of the ramp/corner alternative start to Fiorellini
is **Rebus Gravitazionale**   65m 5c. From a stance above the corner
the route takes a diagonally leftward line following flakes and
cracks.

   Two new climbs take the smooth wall (Parete Liscia) between
CL and Presentimento. Following lines of closely set peg-bolts, the
left is said to be 5c/6a, the right 5b.

191

BALMANOLESCA

This recently developed wall of excellent gneiss offers superb crack-climbing very much to the British taste. Although not a major area, its roadside access and sunny quick-drying nature make it a valuable venue for a one or two day stop-off when entering or leaving Italy via the Simplon Pass (2 hours/60 miles from the Handegg/Grimsell areas). Our visit in late August of '87 took place after one of the worst periods of weather to be recorded in the Alpine regions of Northern Italy and Switzerland. The evening we arrived at Balmanolesca the cliff resembled a waterfall, but due to the overhangs above there were still some lower pitches dry enough to climb. The next morning the flow of water had abated a little but most pitches were still saturated. As the day went on, the hot sun did its work and by late afternoon the cliff was transformed, for with the exception of two or three first pitches and a few upper ones, the cliff was almost completely dry.

Although very close to the road, the cliff is screened by ruined houses and trees so that road noise is virtually unnoticeable.

Access and Approach
1.   From Switzerland via the Simplon Pass. About one mile after the border-post at Gondo are two short road tunnels. One hundred metres after the second tunnel is an uninhabited yellow house on the left-hand side of the road - 'Camping Simplon - Snack Bar' painted on both sides. One hundred metres further on is a group of similarly deserted houses. A track leads through these past a large group of beehives to the foot of the cliff.
2.   From Italy. Driving up from the south or east (Como, Lago di Maggiore etc.) pass through Domodossola (supermarkets etc.) and continue towards the Passo del Sempione (Simplon Pass) to the village of Varzo (665m). The ruined buildings mentioned above will be seen on the right, just under a mile after Varzo.

Camping etc.
The ruined hamlet which has given the cliff its name was con-

structed early this century to house the workers engaged in the long and arduous construction of the Simplon railway tunnel. BEWARE: the buildings may look sound from the outside, but the floors are in an advanced state of decay. Do not enter! There is a good flat area of grass around the yellow house and we had no problems in making an overnight camp midweek. It would also be possible to bivouac in cars near the foot of the crag.

There are a number of small *pensione* and *alberghi* in nearby Varzo, as well as several pizzerias and restaurants.

Guidebooks
Le Guide di Alp - Luoghi della Libera Vol.1 pub. Alp '87. (A gazeteer of climbing areas in north-western Italy.)

Local activist and guide Roberto Pe is preparing a guidebook to the Val d'Ossola area.

Descent
The descent is usually by abseil, except for routes which continue to the middle ledge, in these cases follow the ledge systems right-wards to descend (except for Camino - go off left). All routes are well equipped with spits and chains for stances/abseils, but as the bolts are often well-spaced it is worthwhile carrying Rocks and Friends on most routes. All the routes have their names painted below, and are from left to right:

Il Camino - the obvious chimney line well to the left. Three pitches of 4c, 6a, 5b.

I Quattro Tiri 100m 6a. (Pe & Albert).
The superb crack-line left of Camino reaches the middle ledge by 4 pitches of 5c, 5b, 6a and 5a.

Tostopane 6a. A steep 1 pitch crack.

Il Traversino 5a. The obvious rightward trending flakes lead in two pitches to an abseil point reached more directly by:

Mister Bluff 30m 6a. (Pe & Pe). The slab.

Gufo Triste 30m 6c. A short crack leads to a bolted pillar.

The last three routes can all be used as variation starts to the continuation pitches of: **Tom Tom Club** 15m 6a. (Zanola, R. Pe). The steep wall above and left of the stance.

I Diedri/Tummistufli 80m 5c, 5c, 6a. (Dell'Ava & Pe). A shallow peapod leads to a steep corner crack, continue by a second corner then a thin overhanging crack.

Re Azul is a thin finger crack to the right with a boulder problem start on shotholes (7a?).

Il Sentiero degli Gnomi   45m E3 5c
   Pe & Dell'Ava
1.   30m 5a. Follow the huge flake rightwards to a flared chimney. Climb this in a spectacular position to gain a belay chain on the lip of the roof. (This pitch forms a superb HVS in its own right.)
2.   15m 5c. A crack leads up rightwards to the main roof. Overcome this by a crack running leftwards. Abseil off or continue by:

Balmanolescente   40m 6a, 6c - the slabby wall above and left. Or the unpronounceable **Spluncheiduk**   6a to the right.

La Vastrap is the short slab pitch to the second bolt of Gnomi. Unfortunately you can scarcely miss the name.

Moby Dyck   35m 6a: the compelling (?) off-width - move left above to belay as for Gnomi.

Jean Jacques de la Verdure(6a) gains the sloping ledge on the right to climb the thin impending crack above. Traverse left to belay as above.

Canne d'Organo   30m HVS/E1 5a/b or 100m E3 5c
   Pe, Biselli, Zanolo & Dell'Ava
The aptly named organ pipes have two variant starts well worth climbing in their own right. The left is HVS 5a, the right E1 5b. To continue, climb through the roof above by a leftward leading crack (5c), two more chimney pitches (5b, 5a) lead to the middle ledge.

   Manuela is a new route up the arête to the right, whereas the next crack system is **Banana Nostranna**   25m 6b (moving left to belay and abseil as for Manuela). Ten metres to the right is a very obvious American-style crack system - **Lasciate Ogni Speranza**   80m 6a, 6a, 5a.

OTHER POSSIBILITIES

Although the major crack-lines have now been climbed, numerous variants still await ascents and attention will obviously turn more to the slabs and walls between - not to mention a number of other easily accessible cliffs visible from the road.

Gulliver
Just south of Domodossola is the straggling village of Villadossola. Entering this from the south, an area of quarries with a clean pillar on the right is clearly visible to the left above the main road. Turn up a minor road towards these and park beneath the pillar. Either scramble up large quarried blocks or (better) walk 100m left and return along the quarry track to the foot of the pillar. The classic line of the pillar is **Gulliver** (80m E1 5b) following the central crack-line in three pitches of 5a, 5b, 5a. Left is **Nadia** VS, and to the right the sustained slabs of **Tiziana/Aristotele** 5b, 6b. The smaller pillar to the right gives **Pilastrino** 5c, and there are a number of other bolt lines. With the proximity of the road the ambience leaves something to be desired, but it could be a useful spot in the event of bad weather at the higher Balmanolesca.

For those interested in exploring new areas for themselves, **Rivasco** - a pillar of good gneiss above the village of the same name in the Val Formazza (the upper part of Val d'Ossola) though somewhat remote is said to be worth a visit. A number of other cliffs exist in the same area.

On the Swiss side of the border the rock around Gondo has to be seen to be believed. Unfortunately there is little information available.

GLOSSARY OF ITALIAN CLIMBING TERMS

Aderenza - friction
Albero - tree
Alto - high
Anello - ring
Appiglio - handhold
Appoggiato - leaning
Approccio - approach
Arrampicata libera - free climbing
Assicuriazione - protection
Attacco - start
Attrezzatura - equipment

Bagnato - wet
Basso - low
Bianco - white
Blocco - block
Blocco incastrato - jammed block
Bosco - wood
Buco/chi - hole/holes

Calcare - limestone
Camino - chimney
Campanile - tower (lit. bell-tower)
Canale/Canalone - gully or couloir
Catena - chain
Cengia/Cengetta - ledge
Chiodo - peg or bolt
Chiodo a pressione - peg-bolt
Chiodo espansione - expansion bolt
Clessidra - thread
Colatoio - gully
Consigliabile - recommended
Corda - rope (sometimes sling)
Corda doppia - abseil
Cordino - sling
Corto - short

Dado/i - nut/s
Destra - right
Diedro - corner or groove
Discesa - descent
Dislivello - vertical height of climb

Erba/oso - grass/grassy
Esposto - exposed

Facile - easy
Faticoso - strenuous
Fessura - crack
Fettucce - slings
Filo - edge
Fisso - fixed

Gran/Grande/Grosse - large
Ghiaione - scree
Giallo/Giallastro - yellow/yellowish
Gola - narrow gorge
Gradino - rock step (or foothold)
Gradoni - large rock steps
Grigio - grey
Grotta - cave

Incastro - jamming
Inizio - start

Lama - flake
Largo - wide
Libero/a - free
Liscio/Lucido - smooth or polished
Lunghezza - pitch

Magnesite - chalk
Marcio - rotten or loose (rock etc.)
Marmo - marble
Masso - block
Masso incastrato - chockstone
Materiale - equipment
Moschettone - karabiner
Muro - wall

Nicchia - niche or recess
Nero/Nerastro - black/blackish

Parete - wall or face
Pancia - belly or bulge
Piccolo/a - small
Pilastro - pillar/buttress

Placca/Placche - slab/s

Rampa - ramp
Rifugio - hut
Rinvii - runners i.e. quick draws
Ripido - steep
Roccia - rock
Rosso/astro - red/reddish

Scendere - to descend
Sconsigliabile - not recommended
Sentiero - path
Sinistra - left
Sopra - above
Sosta - stance
Sostenuto - sustained
Sotto - below
Spalla/Spallone - shoulder
Sperone - spur
Spit - expansion bolt
Spuntone - spike

Staccato/a - detached (flake etc.)
Staffa - etriers
Strapiombo - overhang
Stretto - narrow
Strozzatura - narrowing
Svilluppo - length of climb

Terrazzo - terrace
Tetto - roof
Tiro - pitch
Torre - tower
Traverso - traverse

Uscita - exit or finish

Via - route
Via Normale - normal route

Zoccolo - easy rocks below climbing proper - lit. base or plinth (Dolomites)

GLOSSARY OF ENGLISH CLIMBING TERMS

Above - sopra
Abseil - corda doppia
Approach - approccio

Below - sotto
Black/ish - nero/astro
Block - blocco/masso
Bolt - spit/chiodo espansione
Bulge - pancia
Buttress - pilastro

Cave - grotta
Chain - catena
Chalk - magnesite
Chimney - camino
Chockstone - masso incastrato
Climb - via
Climbing - arrampicata
Corner - diedro
Crack - fessura

Descend - scendere
Descent - discesa
Detached - staccato

Easy - facile
Edge - filo
Equipment - materiale
Etriers - staffa
Excellent - eccellente
Exit - uscita
Exposed - esposto

Face - parete
Fine - bello
Fingery - di dita
Fixed - fisso
Flake - lama
Foothold (or step) - gradino
Free - libero
Free Climbing - arrampicata libera
Friction - aderenza

Gorge - gola

Grass/y - erba/oso
Grey - grigio
Groove - dierdo
Gully - canale

Hard - duro/difficile
High - alto
Hold - appiglio
Hole - buco
Hut - Rifugio

Jamming - incastro
Jammed block - blocco incastrato

Karabiner/Krab - moschettone

Large - grosso
Leaning - appoggiato
Ledge - cengia
Left - sinistra
Length (of climb) - svilluppo
Limestone - calcare
Loose/rotten - marcio
Low - basso

Marble - marmo

Narrow - stretto
Narrowing - strozzatura
Niche - nicchia
Nut - dado

Overhang - strapiombo
Overhanging - strapiombante

Path - sentiero
Peg - chiodo
Peg-bolt - chiodo a pressione
Pillar - pilastro
Pitch - tiro
Polished - liscio
Protection - assicuriazione

Quick draws - rinvii

Ramp - rampa

Recommended - consigliabile
Red/dish - rosso/astro
Right - destra
Rock - roccia
Roof - tetto
Route - via
Runners - dadi, rinvii, ecc.

Scree - ghiaione
Short - corto
Shoulder - spalla
Slab - placca
Slings - fettuce
Small - piccolo
Smooth - liscio
Spike - spuntone
Spur - sperone
Stance - sosta

Start - inizio/attacco
Steep - ripido
Strenuous - faticoso
Superb - magnifico
Sustained - sostenuto

Terrace - terrazzo
Thread - clessidra
Tower - torre/campanile
Traverse - traverso
Tree - albero

Wall - parete/muro
Wet - bagnato
White - bianco
Wide - largo
Wood - bosco

Yellow/ish - giallo/astro

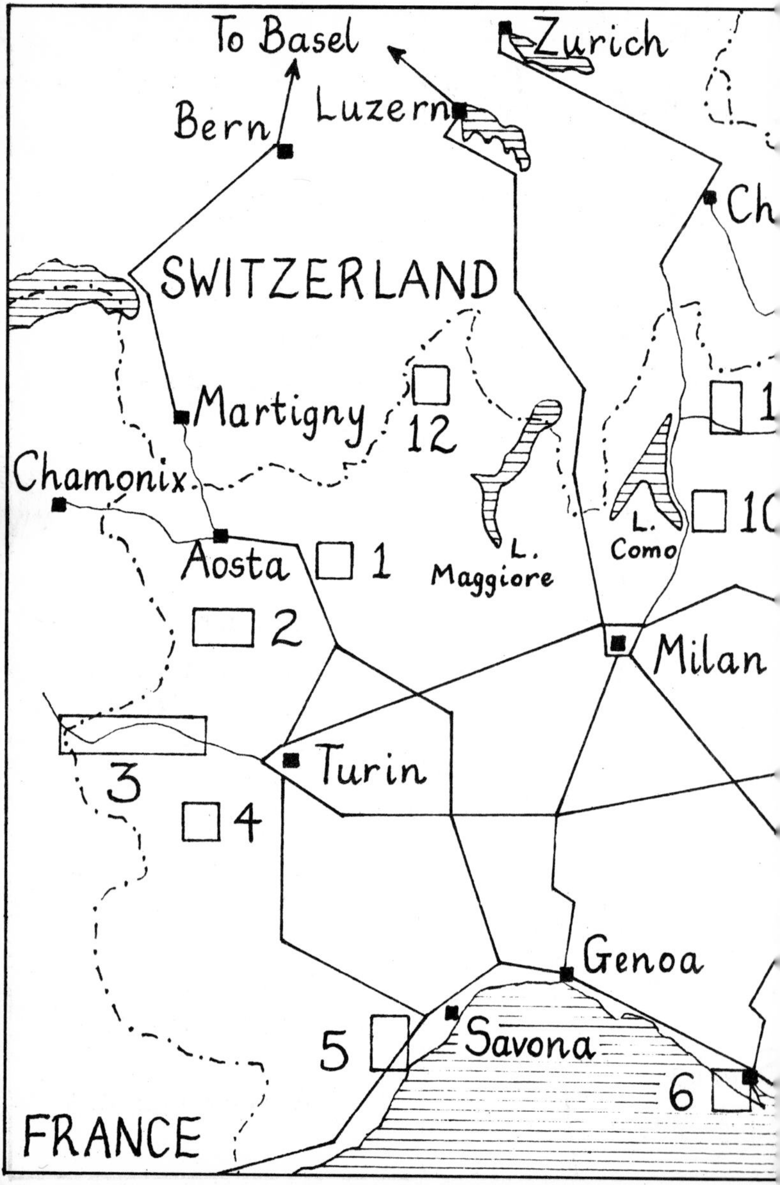

To Basel
Zurich
Bern
Luzern
SWITZERLAND
Martigny
12
Chamonix
Aosta
1
L. Maggiore
L. Como
Milan
2
Turin
3
4
Genoa
Savona
5
6
FRANCE